How to Train Your
English
Springer Spaniel

liz palika

Photo by Isabelle Francais

ENGLISH SPRINGER SPANIEL

Photos by the author unless
otherwise credited.

The Publisher would like to thank all the owners of the dogs in this book, including Doris Cunningham, Joanne Flass, Terri Gainetti, Gail Jackson, Kathy Kirk, Alison McCallum, Tracy Monahan, John Naimo, Libby O'Donnell, Robert Proctor, and Mike Turpen.

© T.F.H. Publications, Inc.

Distributed in the UNITED STATES to the Pet Trade by T.F.H. Publications, Inc., 1 TFH Plaza, Neptune City, NJ 07753; on the Internet at www.tfh.com; in CANADA by Rolf C. Hagen Inc., 3225 Sartelon St., Montreal, Quebec H4R 1E8; Pet Trade by H & L Pet Supplies Inc., 27 Kingston Crescent, Kitchener, Ontario N2B 2T6; in ENGLAND by T.F.H. Publications, PO Box 74, Havant PO9 5TT; in AUSTRALIA AND THE SOUTH PACIFIC by T.F.H. (Australia), Pty. Ltd., Box 149, Brookvale 2100 N.S.W., Australia; in NEW ZEALAND by Brooklands Aquarium Ltd., 5 McGiven Drive, New Plymouth, RD1 New Zealand; in SOUTH AFRICA by Rolf C. Hagen S.A. (PTY.) LTD., P.O. Box 201199, Durban North 4016, South Africa; in JAPAN by T.F.H. Publications, Japan—Jiro Tsuda, 10-12-3 Ohjidai, Sakura, Chiba 285, Japan. Published by T.F.H. Publications, Inc.

MANUFACTURED IN THE
UNITED STATES OF AMERICA
BY T.F.H. PUBLICATIONS, INC.

Contents

INTRODUCTION

Gunner, an English Springer Spaniel, is owned by Jan Flagg of Oceanside, California. At almost nine years old, Gunner is beginning to show his age, with some silver and white hairs infiltrating his previously dark liver markings. However, Gunner is still a very well-behaved dog during his regularly scheduled visits to a local Alzheimer's facility. He sits close to a frail, elderly woman and rests his head on her leg so that she can easily reach him. He holds still as she strokes his long ears, and when her shaking hand comes a bit too close to his eyes he doesn't move away, he simply closes his eyes.

His owner says, "Gunner always enjoys his visits. Of course he loves being the center of attention and getting all the petting, but he is also incredibly gentle and patient with the people he is visiting."

Gunner's owner is also involved with Springer rescue. She helps find homes for Springers that can no longer remain in their original homes. It is a time-consuming, often frustrating volunteer activity that she does out of love for the breed. Springers are often

Springers are lively and spirited dogs that make a wonderful addition to any family.

springer spaniel

Like most dogs, Springers love the outdoors. There are many outside activities that you and your Springer can do together.

available for adoption for many reasons, but the most common one is that the dogs' original owners had no idea what Springers were really like before purchasing one. Many didn't realize how much grooming the dogs need, how much exercise the dogs require, or that Springers need training to become good friends and companions.

I see many different breeds (and mixtures of breeds) in my training classes. When Springers are brought into class, it is usually because the dogs are very active—often out of control—and the owners are desperate to do "something!" With some training and guidance on what makes Springers "tick," we can usually salvage the relationship. However, it would be much easier if people understood what Springers are like prior to adding one to the family.

In this book, I will give owners and prospective owners of Springers important and effective information about training this breed. Springers are good-hearted dogs and they're fun to do things with. With training and some help from their owners, Springers can be wonderful friends, partners, and companions.

SELECTING
the Right Dog for You

WHAT ARE ENGLISH SPRINGER SPANIELS?

In the Beginning

Spaniels originated in Spain as hunting dogs. During their conquests of Europe, the Romans took these Spanish dogs with them. The dogs then spread throughout Europe and the British isles and were used by the residents for a variety of hunting purposes, primarily to flush birds. These dogs all shared some traits, including the pendulous ears and long, silky coat, but other characteristics varied over hundreds of years as the dogs were interbred with resident hunting dogs.

The first written evidence of spaniels as a type of hunting dog occurred in 17 AD. An entry in an Irish king's ledger recorded the gift of a water spaniel. As spaniels became a part of their new regions, they developed into several different types and, gradually, into breeds.

The Springers were originally known as Norfolk spaniels. Taller than other spaniels, these dogs were not uniform in coat type and color. Some had curly coats, some silky straight, some

English Springer Spaniels originated in Spain and were used as hunting dogs, primarily to flush birds.

Photo by Isabelle Francais

Known for their expert hunting abilities, Springers acquired their name by jumping or "springing" on birds from their hiding places.

liver and white, and others red and white. In 1902, the Kennel Club of Great Britain separated the Springer Spaniels by appearance. If the dogs were red and white, they were classified as Welsh Springer Spaniels, and if the dogs were liver and white, they were English Springer Spaniels. This separation still applies today.

The English Springer Spaniel was recognized by the American Kennel Club (AKC) in the early 1900s but really didn't gain popularity until the 1920s. The first conformation show was held in 1922. Shortly thereafter, the English Springer Spaniel Field Trial Association was recognized by the AKC. The members of this club participated in both field trials and conformation shows, often hunting with the dog on Saturday and showing him in conformation the next day.

WHY "SPRINGER?"

"Springer" is a term that refers to this breed's method of flushing birds from their hiding places by springing, or jumping on them. This movement in the field became so identified with these particular spaniels that it became their breed name.

The English Springer Spaniel Today

There are 17 breeds of spaniel today, including the English Springer. This is a medium-sized breed, with males standing 20 inches tall at the shoulder and bitches (females) standing an inch shorter. The weight varies depending on the dog's condition, but a well-muscled male that is 20 inches tall will weigh about 50 pounds. A well-muscled bitch that is an inch shorter will weigh about 40 pounds.

tall. The Springer's head is strong without appearing heavy, and the muzzle is about half the width of the head. The eyes should be medium-sized, oval, and dark, with the color harmonizing with the coat color. The eyes should convey alertness, kindness, and trust. The Springer's ears are set on a level with the eye on the side of the skull. The ear flaps are

The Springer's coat is one of his most defining features. The silky outercoat is of medium length and can be slightly wavy or flat. Colors range from white to black with various markings.

The general appearance of the dog is one of athleticism—this is a dog that should be able to hunt all day long. The body, from the point of the shoulder to the point of the hips, is slightly longer than the dog is

long and wide, and when held forward, they will reach to the end of the nose.

The Springer's coat is two-layered, with an undercoat that makes the dog waterproof and a silky outercoat. The outercoat

A handsome dog, the English Springer Spaniel has an athletic build and an alert, kind expression. Overall, they should appear well balanced, strong, and healthy.

Photo by Isabelle Francais

springer spaniel

is of medium length and can be flat or slightly wavy. The ears, chest, legs, and belly have a longer, feathery coat. On the head, front of the forelegs, and below the hocks on the rear legs, the coat is shorter and fine.

The Springer is an energetic and curious dog that enjoys doing various activities with his owner.

Although most people recognize a liver-and-white dog as a Springer, six color combinations are actually accepted:
- White with liver markings
- White with black markings
- Liver with white markings
- Liver with tan-and-white markings
- Black with white markings
- Black with tan-and-white markings.

In overall appearance, a Springer should convey the impression of being well balanced, strong, and athletic— a working dog.

Temperament

If you want a dog that will play Frisbee™ with you, that will run along the beach chasing sand crabs and seagulls, and that will eagerly accompany you on hikes in the woods, then a Springer is the dog for you. Springers are active, curious, and playful and want to be in the center of everything that's going on. Springers are not reserved, shy, or introverted. The breed as a whole is extroverted.

Benjamin Hart, DVM, and Lynette Hart, in their book *The Perfect Puppy,* say of Springers, "The Springer is the second most playful of all breeds (second only to the Irish Setter) and ranks very high in obedience training. With these traits, it has much of what people look for in a family pet, particularly if they are looking for a fairly lively pet."

The Harts add a word of qualification, however, "The Springer's above-average level of destructiveness is a trait you may want to note with caution." With most breeds, destructiveness (such as chewing up shoes or the garden hose) is generally associated with puppyhood and thought to disappear with maturity. However, the Springer's liveliness, playfulness, and tendency toward destructive behavior go hand in hand. These are traits that can last long into adulthood. Another trait that can accompany these traits is excessive barking. Springers can sometimes be problem barkers.

Springers are generally good family dogs, are not particularly dominant, and are usually good with children. They do bark when people approach the house or yard but are not aggressive watchdogs. Springers thrive with training and are quite intelligent—the more you do with a Springer, the more the dog will like it!

A Word of Warning

Although Springers may seem like the perfect dog for an active family (and most of the time they are), there is a problem that some Springers carry—a genetic predisposition to rage syndrome. Rage syndrome manifests itself as sudden, uncontrolled aggression, sometimes toward people—including the dog's owners. The rage may also cause the dog to attack inanimate objects,

including anything in front of them—the walls, a sofa, a car—or, unfortunately, family pets or other animals.

Karen Overall, an animal behaviorist, describes rage syndrome in this way: "The dog will be uncontrollably aggressive—you could hit him over the head with a two-by-four and he wouldn't notice you were there. And then it turns off just as suddenly." Overall emphasizes that dogs afflicted with rage syndrome are "extremely, extremely dangerous."

Lively and good-natured, the Springer is a popular choice among families. They are well behaved around children and rank very high in their ability to be obedience trained.

springer spaniel

The syndrome was originally identified in the early 1970s, although reports of sudden outbursts of aggressive behavior in Springers had been reported earlier. Reputable breeders have been working to identify the breeding lines that carry this problem, and prior to purchasing any Springer, you should ask the breeder about it.

IS A SPRINGER THE RIGHT DOG FOR YOU?

Evaluating Your Personality and Lifestyle

A healthy Springer can live 12 to 14 years, so the decision to add a Springer to your family is not one to be taken lightly. This is a 14-year commitment, and Springers are intelligent, affectionate, loyal dogs with some specific needs. A good dog/owner match is made when each can satisfy the other's needs.

Being the center of a dog's world can be thrilling to some people but overwhelming to others. Springers are very people-oriented and will want to be close to you as much as possible. When you sit down, your Springer will want to lie at (or on!) your feet. When you leave the room, your Springer will follow you. Obviously, having a dog with you 24 hours a day is

Springers are very people-oriented and like to spend quality time with their owners, even if it's just relaxing in the afternoon.

Photo by Isabelle Francais

springer spaniel

impossible for most people. However, if you want a Springer, you will need to provide as much companionship as possible.

Are you an active person? Do you like to run, jog, hike, or ride

Do you enjoy grooming a dog? Grooming a Springer consists of brushing, combing, de-matting, bathing, drying, and trimming that beautiful coat. Springers do need daily grooming (a minimum of

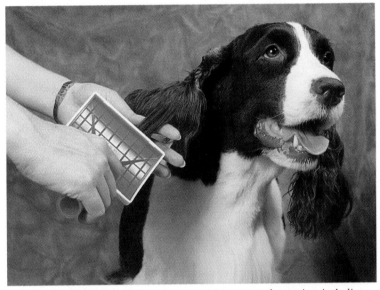

An English Springer Spaniel requires a certain amount of grooming, including brushing, combing, de-matting, bathing, drying, and trimming the coat.

Photo by Isabelle Francais

your bike? Springers like to be active, and if you're looking for a dog to do things with you, a Springer might be the right choice.

If you are not quite so active, you might want to think about adopting an older Springer that will enjoy going for a walk rather than a fast-paced run and that will enjoy quiet times at home.

brushing, combing, and de-matting) to keep their coat healthy, so if you don't enjoy grooming, don't get a Springer.

The Springer's Needs

All dogs have some specific needs that may clash or coincide with yours. It's important to think about the dog's needs prior to adding him to your family.

First of all, your companionship is very important. Springers are very much family dogs, and companionship with their people is critical for a good relationship. Springers also need training, because they are not born knowing how to be good family dogs.

You will also need to provide your dog with a

Exercise and play are vital to your Springer's overall health. It allows him to relax and work off any stress that he might be feeling.

securely fenced yard or dog run. Springers are not the escape artists some other breeds can be, but they are curious dogs. If it's too easy to get out of the yard, they will.

Your Springer will also need regular exercise. If you like to run or jog, that's great. A healthy young Springer can learn how to run next to your bicycle, too. One walk a day cannot be considered nearly enough exercise for a Springer.

Your Springer also needs daily playtime. Although play can be exercise, it is important emotionally for Springers. Your dog needs time to chase a ball, play hide-and-seek with you, or chase birds in the field while you cheer him on. Playtime gives you and your dog time to relax and laugh together.

SELECTING THE RIGHT DOG

Male or Female?

There are a lot of myths about the personality traits of both males and females. Ultimately, it depends on the personality of the individual dog. Spayed bitches (females) and neutered dogs (males) are usually a little calmer. Spaying and neutering removes the sexual hormones and the sexual tension that can accompany those hormones. To be a good pet and companion, your Springer doesn't need those hormones anyway.

Springers vary in size by sex, and this could affect your

Photo by Isabelle Francais

Puppies require a lot of work, time, and patience. Make sure that you can provide these things before you take a puppy home.

springer spaniel

choice. A male Springer is a little taller and heavier than a female and is often more muscular, with a bigger chest and shoulders.

Male Springers can be a little more reactive than females, more stimulated by things going on around them. Females generally accept training better than males. However, these are generalizations. Each dog (and bitch) is an individual and may vary from these tendencies.

If you decide that a Springer puppy is not the best choice for you, local animal shelters and newspaper advertisements are some of the sources from which you can adopt an older Springer.

What Age?

Puppies are adorable. However, when you add a puppy to your family it's just like having a new baby. Puppies, like babies, eat often, sleep a lot, relieve themselves often, and demand a lot of your time. As your puppy grows, he will become an integral part of your family. By the time your Springer is fully grown (about two years of age), your dog will have

become a good friend and companion.

If you don't have the time or patience to raise a puppy, that doesn't mean you can't get a dog. Older puppies and adult Springers can be great pets, too, and are often available for adoption.

Adopting a Springer that is not a young puppy might have some drawbacks, however. The process can be compared to buying a used car— sometimes you get a gem and sometimes you get a lemon. You often have no information about the dog's previous life—how was he treated? Does he have any training? Where did he come from? Is there rage syndrome in his family? Most of the time, there is very little known about his health history.

In addition, newly adopted dogs must also have time to settle into their new homes and to adjust emotionally and physically. Changing homes can be very traumatic. A newly adopted Springer may be very clingy and may show signs of separation anxiety when left alone. Usually, these behaviors will decrease as the dog settles into the new home, bonds with his new owners, and feels more comfortable.

Finding an Adult Dog

If you have decided that you don't have the time for a puppy, and an adult dog would be a better choice for you, you can look for an adult Springer in a few different places. Dogs found through classified advertisements are usually being given up by their owners, and in this situation, you can ask some questions. Why are they giving up the dog? Where did they get the dog? Is the dog originally from a reputable breeder who was knowledgeable about rage syndrome? Has the dog been spayed or neutered and had all the necessary vaccinations?

You can also look for a dog through the local humane society or animal shelter. You will rarely be able to find out anything about the background of these dogs, however, as some might be strays. Privacy laws also usually forbid the shelters from giving the prospective owner any past information—other than vaccination records and basic facts about how the dog came to the shelter.

RESCUE GROUPS

Many breed clubs sponsor or run breed rescue groups. These organizations screen the dogs they take in for adoption, which can be beneficial to you. The dogs will have been vaccinated, spayed, or neutered and should be healthy. In addition, a breed expert will have evaluated the dog for training (or lack thereof) and behavioral problems. Rage syndrome will still be an unknown, as dogs with rage rarely give any behavioral signs prior to an attack. (Dogs known to have rage are never put up for adoption.) To find a local Springer rescue group, ask for information from your local shelter or humane society.

Evaluating an Adult Dog

Once you have found an adult Springer, how do you know this is the right dog for you? First of all, do you like him? Your feelings for the dog are certainly going to play a big part in your relationship with him, and if you don't like the dog, you should probably keep looking. However, if you *do* like the dog, don't say yes just because of that. There is more to the decision-making process than just liking the dog.

Do you know why the owner gave up this dog? Sometimes dogs are given up through no fault of their own—perhaps the owner was transferred overseas or passed away. However, if the dog was given up because of behavior problems, you should know about that, especially if he was given up because of aggressive behavior.

Has the dog had any training? Is the dog housetrained? These are important issues, because even if you are willing to train the dog, housetraining a previously untrained adult Springer can be quite an undertaking.

What is the dog's personality like? Springers are usually happy dogs. However, many things can affect a dog's personality, including poor breeding practices and a lack of socialization as a puppy. When you whistle, does the dog cock his head to the side and look at you, wagging the stub of his tail? Great! If he looks sideways at you, slinks, or bares his throat, be careful—this dog is worried or scared, and a fearful dog can bite. Be careful, too, if the dog stands on his tiptoes and stares you in the eye. This is challenging you and could be a problem.

Ideally, you want a dog that is happy to see you without showing too much worry or fearfulness and without showing any aggression. You want a dog that is housetrained and has hopefully had some obedience training. Make sure you can live with the dog's behavior problems for the time being, until the dog has settled in and you can start training.

Although Springer puppies are adorable, adults can be just as charming. If you are going to adopt an older Springer, spend enough time with the dog to make sure that your personalities match.

Finding a Puppy

If you have the time and patience to raise a puppy, you will want to find a reputable breeder. Breeder referrals come from many different sources. A neighbor walking a healthy, well-behaved Springer might refer you to her dog's breeder. Your veterinarian might have a client who consistently raises healthy puppies. Many of the national dog magazines have ads for breeders. You may also want to attend a dog show in your area and talk to people there.

Once you have the names of a few breeders, call and ask for an appointment to meet with them. At the meeting, ask a few questions: "Are you active in dog shows, field trials, or dog sports?" If the breeder shows her dogs in conformation dog shows, they are probably good physical representatives of the breed. If the breeder participates in field trials, the dogs have the hunting instincts they were bred to have. Unless you plan on competing in field trials yourself, these dogs might be a little intense for pets, however, so talk to the breeder. If the breeder participates in dog sports, her dogs are probably quite trainable and physically sound.

"Do you belong to the national or regional Springer clubs?" Clubs routinely publish newsletters and magazines containing articles of interest to Springer owners and breeders, including the most recent information about health and genetics.

"Can you provide me with a list of references?" Of course,

Finding the right puppy to match your personality and lifestyle is important. Once you find a reputable breeder, make sure to ask plenty of questions about his or her dogs and the facilities in which the puppies are raised.

Photo by Isabelle Francais

she will give you a list of people she knows are happy with her dogs, but that's okay. You can still ask them some questions. "Did the breeder deliver the puppy's paperwork?" "Was the puppy healthy?" "Would you buy a puppy from her again?"

Caring breeders will ask you just as many questions as you ask them. They want to know you are the right person for one of their puppies. Don't get defensive, just answer the questions honestly. If by some chance the breeder says that her puppies are not the right dogs for you, listen to her. After all, she knows her dogs better than anyone.

If you have a quiet and easy-going personality, a submissive Springer would be a better choice than one that has a more dominant personality.

Photo by Isabelle Francais

Evaluating a Puppy

Each puppy has his or her own personality, and finding the right personality to match yours is sometimes a challenge. For example, if you are outgoing, extroverted, and active, a quiet, withdrawn, and submissive puppy will not fit well into your family. On the other hand, that quiet puppy would do quite well in a home with a less active, quiet person.

When you go to look at a puppy, there are a few things you can do to help evaluate his personality. Take the puppy away from his mother and littermates, preferably to another room. Set him down on the floor and walk away from him. Squat down and call him. An outgoing, extroverted puppy will come happily and climb into your lap. If you stand up and walk away, the extrovert will follow you, trying to get underfoot. If you throw a piece of crumpled paper, he will charge after it. He may then shake the paper, "killing" it, or he may bring it back to you. This Springer would do well with an owner who is just as much an extrovert as he is. He will need training to learn some rules and self-control, as well as lots of exercise and a job to occupy his mind.

Photo by Isabelle Francais

A dog is a lifelong commitment. Give your Springer puppy all the love, affection, and care that he needs in order to grow into a healthy and well-behaved adult.

The quieter puppy will follow you when you walk away but may do a belly crawl or roll over and bare his belly. When you walk away again, he will watch you but may be hesitant to follow. When you throw the paper, he will probably go after it but may hesitate to bring it back. This puppy will need a quiet owner, gentle handling, and positive training.

These two puppies are the extreme of Springer personalities—most Springers are somewhere in between these two extremes. Try to find a puppy with a personality that will be compatible with your own. Do not choose a quiet, submissive puppy out of sympathy, unless that personality is best for your family. On the other hand, don't choose the boldest puppy, either, unless you are prepared to deal with that personality for the next 14 years.

CHOOSE WISELY

Adding a dog to your family should be a time of anticipation and excitement, but to make it work, it should also be a time of research, careful thought, and preparation. Without planning, the entire process could easily turn into a nightmare. This dog will be your friend and companion for the next 14 years, so choose wisely.

Canine
DEVELOPMENT
Stages

UNDERSTANDING THE ANCIENT DOG OWNER BOND

Archaeologists have found scattered bones, teeth, and primitive artworks to show that dogs or their ancestors have been associated with mankind since at least the end of the last Ice Age. In La Grotte du Lazaret in France, a 125,000-year-old complex of Paleolithic sites, wolf skulls were set at the entrance of each dwelling.

Why? To protect the inhabitants? We don't know. What we can speculate is that wolves, the ancestors of today's dogs, were already becoming important to human culture.

Families and Packs

Most researchers agree that the ancestors of today's dogs were wolves. They disagree on which wolves those ancestors were—either the ancestors of today's gray wolves or perhaps

Most English Springer Spaniels feel comfortable and adapt well to large families. This Springer looks perfectly happy surrounded by some of his closest friends.

springer spaniel

Photo by Isabelle Francais

For the first few weeks of a Springer puppy's life, his mother and littermates are the only ones of any significance. A mother's milk provides her newborn with all of the necessary nutrients needed for healthy growth.

a species of wolf that is now extinct. In any event, wolves are social creatures that live in an extended family pack. The pack might consist of a dominant (alpha) male and a dominant (alpha) female. These two are usually the only two that breed. There will also be subordinate males and females, juveniles, and puppies. This is a very harmonious group that hunts together, plays together, defends its territory against intruders, and cares for each other. Discord only occurs when there is a change in the pack order. If one of the leaders becomes disabled, an adult leaves the pack, or a subordinate adult tries to assume dominance, there may be some jockeying around to fill that position.

Many experts feel domesticated dogs adapt so well to our lifestyle because we also live in groups. We call our groups families instead of packs, but they are still a social organization. However, the comparison isn't really accurate, because our families are much more chaotic than the average wolf pack. We are terribly inconsistent with our social rules and rules for behavior. (We let our Springer jump up and paw us when we're in grubby clothes but yell at him when he jumps up on our good clothes.) To the dog, our communication skills are also confusing. Our voice says one thing, while our body language

At the age of five weeks, a puppy begins to recognize people and to respond to individual voices. He is also playing more with his littermates.

says something else. We can say that both dogs and humans live in social groups, and we can use that comparison to understand a little more about our dogs. However, we must also understand that our families are very different from a wolf pack.

FROM BIRTH TO FOUR WEEKS OF AGE

For the first three weeks of life, the family and the pack are unimportant as far as the baby Springer is concerned. The only one of any significance is his mother. She is the key to his survival and the source of food, warmth, and security.

At four weeks of age, the baby Springer's needs are still being met by his mother, but his littermates are becoming more important. His brothers and sisters provide warmth and security when their mother leaves the nest. His curiosity is developing and he will climb on and over his littermates, learning their scent and feel. During this period, he will learn to use his sense of hearing to follow sounds and his sense of vision to follow moving objects.

His mom will also start disciplining the puppies—very gently, of course—and this early discipline is vitally important to the puppies' future acceptance of discipline and training.

The breeder should be handling the puppies now to get them used to gentle handling by people. At this age, the puppies can learn the difference between their mother's touch and gentle handling by people.

WEEKS FIVE THROUGH SEVEN

The young Springer goes through some tremendous changes between five and seven weeks of age. He is learning to recognize people and is starting to respond to individual voices. He is playing more with his littermates, and the wrestling and scuffling teaches each puppy how to get along, how to play, when the play is too rough, when to be submissive, and what to take seriously. His mother's discipline at this stage of development teaches the puppy to accept corrections, training, and affection.

LET THE MOTHER DOG CORRECT

Some inexperienced breeders will stop the mother dog from correcting her puppies, perhaps thinking that the mother dog is impatient, tired, or a poor mother. When the mother dog is not allowed to correct the puppies naturally, the puppies do not learn how to accept discipline and therefore have a hard time later when their new owner tries to establish some rules. Orphaned puppies raised by people suffer from the same problems. The mother dog knows instinctively what to do for her babies, and sometimes a correction—a low growl, a bark, or a snap of the teeth—is exactly what is needed.

The puppies should never be taken from their mother at this stage of development. Puppies taken away now and sent to

new homes may have lasting behavior problems. They often have difficulty dealing with other dogs, may have trouble accepting rules and discipline, and may become excessively shy, aggressive, or fearful.

Photo by Isabelle Francais

Before you introduce your Springer to other people and dogs, make sure he's had all of his necessary vaccinations.

THE EIGHTH WEEK

The eighth week of life is a frightening time for most puppies. Puppies go through several fear periods during their maturation, and this is the first one. Even though this is the traditional time for most puppies to go to their new homes, they would actually benefit by staying with their littermates for one more week. If the puppy leaves the breeder's home during this fear period and is frightened by the car ride home, he may retain that fear of car rides for the rest of his life. In fact, this stress is why so many puppies get carsick. The same applies to the puppy's new home, his first trip to the veterinarian's office, or anything else that frightens him.

WEEKS NINE THROUGH TWELVE

The baby Springer can go to his new home anytime during the ninth and tenth weeks of life. At this age, he is ready to form permanent relationships. Take advantage of this and spend time with your new puppy, playing with him and encouraging him to explore his new world. Teach him his name by calling him in a happy, high-pitched tone of voice. Encourage him to follow you by backing away from him, patting your leg, and calling his name.

Socialization is very important now, too. Socialization is more than simply introducing your puppy to other people, dogs, noises, and sounds. It is making sure your baby Springer is not frightened by these things as you introduce them. For example, once your baby Springer has had some vaccinations (check with your veterinarian), take him with you to the pet store when you go to buy dog food. While there, introduce your puppy to the store clerks, other customers, and even to the store parrot. Your trip there could also include walking up some stairs, walking on slippery floors, and going through an automatic door. All of these things, introduced gradually and with encouragement, and repeated all over town (on different days, of course) add up to a confident, well-socialized puppy.

During this stage of development, your Springer puppy's pack instincts are developing. He is beginning to understand which people belong to his pack or family and which do not. Do not let him growl at visitors during this stage—he is much too young to understand when and how to protect. Instead, stop the growling and let him know that you, as his pack leader, can protect the family.

You can show him his position in the family in several different ways, but one of the easiest is to lay him down, roll him over, and give him a tummy rub. This exercise may seem very simple, but by baring his tummy he is assuming a

Photo by Isabelle Francais

Remember to be consistent with your puppy when enforcing the household rules. If given the chance, new puppies will try to establish a dominant role.

submissive position to you. When his mother corrected him by growling or barking at him, he would roll over and bare his tummy to her, in essence telling her, "Okay! I understand, you're the boss!" When you have him roll over for a tummy rub, you are helping him understand the same message, but you are doing it in a very gentle, loving way.

During this stage of development, discipline is very important. Love, affection, and security are still important, too, of course, but right now your Springer puppy needs to learn that his life is governed by some rules. Don't allow him to do anything now that you won't want him to continue doing later as a full-grown dog.

WEEKS THIRTEEN THROUGH SIXTEEN

From 13 through 16 weeks of age, your Springer puppy will be trying to establish his position in your family pack. If you were able to set some rules in earlier stages of development, this won't be quite so difficult. However, if you cave in to that adorable puppy face, this could be a challenging time!

Consistency in enforcing household rules is very important now, and everyone in the family or household should be enforcing the rules in the same way. Springers are very perceptive, and if your puppy senses a weak link in the chain of command, he will take advantage of it. This doesn't mean he's a bad puppy, it simply means he's a smart puppy.

Dominant personality puppies may start mounting behavior on small children in the family or the puppy's toys. Obviously, this is undesirable behavior and should be stopped immediately—just don't let it happen.

Socialization to other people, friendly dogs, and other experiences should continue throughout this stage of development.

RETRIEVING

Begin retrieving games at 9 to 12 weeks of age. Get your Springer's attention with a toy he likes, and then toss it four to six feet away. When he grabs the toy, call him back to you in a happy tone of voice. Praise him enthusiastically when he brings it back to you. If he runs away and tries to get you to chase him, stand up and walk away, stopping the game completely. Don't chase him! Let him learn now, while he's young, that he must play games by your rules. Chasing a ball or soft flying disc can be great exercise for the puppy, and by teaching him to play by your rules, you'll also set the stage for a sound working relationship later.

WEEKS SEVENTEEN THROUGH TWENTY SIX

Sometime between 17 and 26 weeks of age, most puppies go through another fear period, much like the one they went through at 8 weeks of age. Things the puppy had accepted as normal may suddenly become frightening. A friend's Springer walked into the backyard and began barking fearfully at the picnic table that had been there in the same spot since before the puppy joined the family. It was if the puppy had never noticed it before, and all at once it was very scary.

Make sure you don't reinforce any of these fears. If you pet him or cuddle him and tell him softly, "It's okay, sweetie, don't be afraid," he will assume these are positive reinforcements for his fears. In other words, your puppy will think he was right to be afraid. Instead, walk up to whatever is scaring him, letting him see you touch it, and tell him, "Look at this!" in a happy tone of voice so that he can see the thing he is afraid of really isn't scary at all.

Your Springer's protective instincts will continue to develop through this stage. If your Springer continues to show protectiveness or

Photo by Isabelle Francais

Guidance and discipline are essential factors in your puppy's overall behavior, but he also needs love and affection from the people closest to him.

aggression (with growling, snarling, barking, or raised hackles), interrupt his behavior by turning him away or distracting him. If you encourage this behavior this early, or if you correct it too harshly, you will put too much emphasis on it and your puppy may continue to do it. Too much emphasis this young may result in overprotectiveness or fearfulness in your dog as he grows up. Instead, react with calmness and just stop it from happening.

Springers are not naturally aggressive as adults, although they will bark when people come up to the house or yard. However, at this age, your Springer puppy doesn't know when to bark, growl, or be protective. Instead of letting him take over (and learn bad habits), stop his behavior and let him know you are in charge.

THE TEENAGE MONTHS

The teenage months in a dog's life are very much like the teenage years in a human's life. Human adolescents are feeling strong and striving to prove their ability to take care of themselves. They want to be independent, yet they still want the security of home. These two conflicting needs seem to drive some teens (and their parents) absolutely crazy!

Dogs can be very much the same way. Springers in adolescence push the boundaries of their rules, trying to see if you really will enforce those rules. Most Springer owners say their dogs in this stage of growing up act "too full of themselves!"

The teenage stage in Springers usually hits at about 12 months of age, although it's not unusual to see it happen a month or two earlier. You'll know when it happens. One day you will ask your previously well-trained dog to do something he knows very well, such as sit, and he'll look at you as if you're nuts. He's never heard that word before in his life, and even if he had, he still wouldn't do it!

Other common behaviors include a regression in social skills. Your previously well-socialized Springer may start barking at other dogs or jumping on people. He may start getting rough with children or chasing the cat.

During this stage of development, you need to consistently enforce social and household rules. If you have already started obedience training, that control will help.

It is important to provide your dog with a nutritionally fortified diet geared toward his stage of life. Look for foods that are naturally preserved, contain no by-products, and are 100 percent guaranteed. Photo courtesy of Midwestern Pet Foods, Inc.

If you haven't started obedience training, do so now—don't wait any longer.

Make sure, too, that your dog regards you as the leader. This is not the time to try to be best friends—that would cause a dominant personality to regard you as weak. Instead, act like the leader. Stand tall when you relate to your dog. Bend over him, not down to him, when you pet him. You should always go first through doorways or up the stairs, making him wait to follow you. You should always eat first before you feed him.

As the leader, you can give him permission to do things. For example, if he goes to pick up a toy for you to throw to him, give him permission to do it, "Good boy to bring me your toy!" If he lies down at your feet (by his own choice), tell him, "Good boy to lie down!" By giving him permission and praising him, you are putting yourself in control, even though he was already doing it of his own accord.

You need to understand that this rebellion is not aimed at you, personally. Your Springer is not doing this to you. Instead, it is a very natural part of growing up—and your Springer *will* grow up, someday.

Obedience training should begin as soon as possible. It's important that your Springer understands that you are the leader.

Adolescence usually only lasts a few months (in dogs, anyway).

GROWING UP

Springers are not usually considered fully mature mentally and physically until they are two years old. And even then, some Springers still act like puppies for even longer. Usually, the females act mature a little earlier than the males.

After the teenage stage but before maturity, your Springer may go through another fear period. This usually hits at about 14 months of age but may be later. Handle this one just like you did the others—don't reinforce your dog's fears. Happily, this is usually the last fear stage your dog will have.

There may be another period of challenging—seeing if you really are the boss—at about two years of age. Treat this as you did the teenage stage: enforce the rules and praise what the dog does right.

Early
PUPPY
Training

HOUSETRAINING

One of the most common methods of housetraining a puppy is paper training. The puppy is taught to relieve himself on newspapers and then, at some point, is retrained to go outside. Paper training teaches the puppy to relieve himself in the house. Is that really what you want your Springer to know?

Teach your Springer what you want him to know now *and* later as an adult. Take him outside to the place where you want him to relieve himself and tell him, "Sweetie, go potty." (Use any word you'll be comfortable saying.) When he has done what he needs to do, praise him.

Don't just open the door and send your puppy outside. How do you know that he has relieved

Paper training is an effective method of housetraining, especially for owners who aren't at home during the day to let their dog outside.

Photo by Isabelle Francais

s p r i n g e r   s p a n i e l

Photo by Isabelle Francais

Housetraining your new puppy can be challenging. Consistency and positive reinforcement can help make the housetraining process a success.

himself? Go out with him so that you can teach him the command, praise him when he does it, and know when he is done and it's safe to let him back inside.

If he doesn't relieve himself when you take him outside, just put him back in his crate for a little while and take him back outside later. Do *not* let him run around the house, even supervised, if he has not relieved himself outside.

Successful housetraining is based on setting your Springer puppy up for success rather than failure. Keep accidents to a minimum and praise him when he does relieve himself in the correct location.

BLANK SLATE

A young puppy's mind is like a newly formatted computer disk. What you teach your English Springer Spaniel puppy in his early months will have bearing on his behavior for the rest of his life. Therefore, it's important to keep in mind a vision of what your Springer will grow up to be. Although Springers are medium-sized dogs (not a large breed), they are strong and athletic. At ten weeks of age, your Springer puppy will enjoy a cuddle on your lap, but will you still want him to do that when he's 50 pounds of muscle and hard elbows? Teach him as a puppy what you want him to do as an adult.

Establishing a routine for your Springer will help him adjust to the new household rules.
Give everyone in the family an assigned role and be consistent.

Establish a Routine

Springers, like many other dogs, are creatures of habit and thrive on a routine. Housetraining is much easier if there is a set routine for eating, eliminating, playing, walking, training, and sleeping. A workable schedule might look like this:

• **6:00 am**—Dad wakes up and takes the puppy outside. After the puppy relieves himself, Dad praises him and brings him inside. Dad fixes the puppy's breakfast, offers him water, and then sends him out in the backyard while he goes to take his shower.

• **7:00 am**—Mom goes outside to play with the puppy for a few minutes before getting ready for work. Just before she leaves, she brings the puppy inside, puts him in his crate, and gives him a treat.

• **11:00 am**—A dog-loving neighbor who is retired comes over. He lets the puppy out of his crate and takes him outside. The neighbor is familiar with the puppy's training, so he praises the puppy when he relieves himself. He throws the ball for the puppy, pets him, and cuddles him. When the puppy is

PUNISHMENT

Do not try to housetrain your puppy by correcting him for relieving himself in the house. If you scold him or rub his nose in his mess, you are not teaching him where he needs to relieve himself—you are instead teaching him that you think going potty is wrong. Since he has to go, he will then become sneaky about it, and you will find puddles and piles in strange places. Keep in mind that the act of relieving himself is very natural; he *has* to do it. Instead of concentrating on correction, emphasize the praise for going in the right place.

The use of a crate is very helpful in the housetraining process. Keeping your Springer inside the crate for short periods of time will help him develop bowel and bladder control.

worn out, he puts him back in his crate and gives him a treat.

• **3:00 pm**—Daughter comes home from school and takes the puppy outside. She throws the ball for the puppy, cleans up the yard a little, and then takes the puppy for a walk. When they get back, she brings the puppy inside to her bedroom while she does her homework.

• **6:00 pm**—Mom takes the puppy outside to go potty, praises him, and then feeds him dinner.

• **8:00 pm**—After Daughter plays with the puppy, she

brushes him and then takes him outside to go potty.

• **11:00 pm**—Dad takes the puppy outside for one last trip before bed.

The schedule you set up will have to work with your normal routine and lifestyle. Just keep in mind that your Springer puppy should not remain in the crate for longer than three to four hours at a time, except during the night. In addition, the puppy will need to relieve himself after waking up, after eating, after playtime, and every three to four hours in between.

CRATE TRAINING

By about five weeks of age, most puppies are starting to toddle away from their mom and littermates to relieve themselves. You can use this instinct to keep the bed clean and to housetrain your Springer puppy, with the help of a crate.

A crate is a plastic or wire travel cage that you can use as your Springer's bed. Many new Springer owners shudder at the thought of putting their puppy in a cage. "I could never do that!" they say. "It would be like putting my children in jail!" A puppy is not a child, however, and he has different needs and instincts. Puppies like to curl up in small, dark places. That's why they like to sleep under the coffee table or a chair.

Because your Springer puppy has an instinct to keep his bed clean, being confined in the crate will help him develop more bowel and bladder control. When he is confined for gradually extended periods of time, he will hold his wastes to avoid soiling his bed. It is your responsibility to make sure he isn't left too long.

The crate will also be your Springer puppy's place of refuge. If he's tired, hurt, or sick, allow him to go back to his crate to sleep or hide. If he's overstimulated or excited, put him back in his crate to calm down.

Because the crate physically confines the puppy, it can also prevent some unwanted behaviors, such as destructive chewing or raiding the trash cans. When you cannot supervise the puppy, or when you leave the house, put him in his crate and he won't be able to get into trouble.

Introducing the Crate

Introduce your puppy to the crate by propping open the door and tossing a treat inside. As you do this, tell your puppy, "Go to bed!" Let him go inside to get the treat, investigate the crate,

and come and go as he wishes. When he's comfortable with that, offer him his next meal in the crate. Once he's in, close the door behind him. Let him out when he's through eating. Offer several meals in the same fashion to show your puppy that the crate is a pretty neat place.

Offer your puppy his meals in the crate. This will help him get used to the new surroundings and show him that good things happen when he's in there.

After your Springer puppy is used to going in and out for treats and meals, start feeding him in his normal place again and go back to offering a treat for going into the crate. Tell him, "Sweetie, go to bed," and then give him his treat.

Don't let your puppy out of the crate for a temper tantrum. If he starts crying, screaming, throwing himself at the door, or scratching at the door, correct him verbally, "No, quiet!" or

Photo by Isabelle Francais

A well-groomed dog is a happy dog, so don't let cumbersome grooming tools stop you from getting the job done. There are compact, lightweight tools available. Photo courtesy of Wahl, USA.

while you do nothing but sleep. In these busy times, that is quality time.

Having you nearby will give your Springer puppy a feeling of security, whereas exiling him to the laundry room or backyard will isolate him. He will be more apt to cry, whine, chew destructively, or get into other trouble because of loneliness and fear.

Having the crate close at night will save you some wear and tear, too. If he needs to go outside during the night (and he may need to for a few weeks), you will hear him whine, and you can let him out before he has an accident. If he's restless or

simply close the door to the room and walk away. If you let him out for a tantrum, you will simply teach him that temper tantrums work. Instead, let him out when you are ready to let him out and when he is quiet.

Crate Location

The ideal place for the crate is in your bedroom, within arm's reach of the bed. This will give your Springer eight uninterrupted hours with you

---

THERE ARE NO ACCIDENTS

If the puppy relieves himself in the house it is not his fault, it's yours. It means the puppy was not supervised well enough, or he wasn't taken outside in time. The act of relieving himself is very natural to the puppy, and the idea that there are certain areas where relieving himself is not acceptable is foreign. His instincts tell him to keep his bed clean, but that's all. You need to teach him where you want him to go and prevent him from going in other places. That requires your supervision.

KEEP WALKING
Do you walk your dog when he has to go potty? Many dog owners live in condos and apartments, and the dog must go for a walk to relieve himself. These dogs often learn that the walk is over once they go potty, and they hold it as long as possible so that the walk continues. To avoid this trap, encourage your puppy to relieve himself right away, praise him, and then continue the walk or outing for a little while afterwards.

bored, you can rap on the top of his crate and tell him to be quiet without getting out of bed.

LIMIT THE PUPPY'S FREEDOM
Many puppies do not want to take the time to go outside to relieve themselves because everything exciting happens in the house. After all, that's where all the family members are. If your Springer puppy is like this, you will find him sneaking off somewhere, behind the sofa or to another room, to relieve himself. By limiting the puppy's

Most dogs don't want to go outside to relieve themselves, because they think that the house is where everything exciting happens. You can help change their mind by going outside with your dog often.

springer spaniel

freedom, you can prevent some of these mistakes. Close bedroom doors and use baby gates across hallways to keep him close. If you can't keep an eye on him, put him in his crate or outside.

PATIENCE, PATIENCE, AND MORE PATIENCE

Springer puppies need time to develop bowel and bladder control. Establish a routine that seems to work well for you and your puppy, and then stick to it. Give your puppy time to learn what you want and time to grow up. If you stick to the schedule, your puppy will progress. However, don't let success go to your head. A few weeks without a mistake doesn't mean your Springer puppy is housetrained, it means your routine is working. Too much freedom too soon will result in problems.

HOUSEHOLD RULES

It's important to start teaching your Springer puppy the household rules as soon as possible. Your eight- to ten-week-old puppy is not too young to learn, and by starting early, you can prevent him from learning bad habits.

When deciding what rules you want him to learn, look at your Springer puppy not as the baby he is now but as the adult he will grow up to be. Are you going to want him up on the furniture when he's 50 pounds of muscle, long legs, hard elbows, and rough paws? Do you want him to jump up on people? Given their own way, all Springers jump up. Do you want him to do that to the neighbor's children or to your grandmother?

Some rules you may want to institute could include teaching your Springer that jumping on people is not allowed, that he must behave when guests come to the house, that he should stay out of the kitchen, that he should leave the trash cans alone, and that he should chew only on his toys.

Teaching your Springer puppy these rules is not difficult. Be very clear with your corrections. When he does something wrong, correct him with your deep, firm tone of voice, "No jump!" When he does something right, use a higher-pitched tone of voice, "Good boy to chew on your toy!" You must be very clear—either something is right or it is wrong, there are no shades of gray in between.

ACCEPTING THE LEASH

Learning to accept the leash can be difficult for some puppies. If your Springer puppy learns to dislike the leash as a young puppy, he may continue to resent it for many years. However, if he learns the leash is a key to more exciting things, he will welcome the leash.

Soon after you bring your puppy home, put a soft buckle collar on his neck. Make sure it's on the leash, feel it tug on his neck, and in doing so will get used to the feel of it.

After two or three short sessions like this, you can then teach your puppy to follow you on the leash. Have a few pieces of a soft, easily chewed treat your puppy enjoys. Hold the

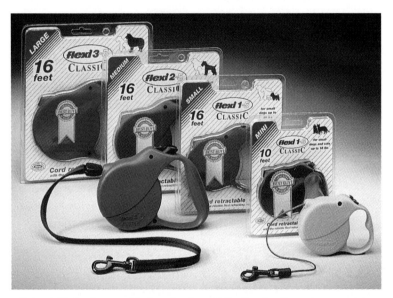

Retractable leashes provide dogs freedom while allowing the owner complete control. Leashes are available in a wide variety of lengths for all breeds of dogs. Photo courtesy of Flexi-USA, Inc.

loose enough to come over his head if he gets tangled up in something. Give him a day or two to get used to the collar. Then, when you are going to be close by and can supervise him, snap the leash onto the collar and let him drag it behind him. As he walks around, he will step leash in one hand and the treats in another. Show him the treat, and back away a few steps as you tell your puppy, "Let's go! Good boy!" When he follows you a few steps, praise him and give him the treat. Springer puppies are usually very food-motivated, and when your puppy learns a treat is being offered, he should follow you with no problem.

Repeat two or three times, and then stop for this training session. Reward your puppy by giving him a tummy rub or throwing the ball a few times.

After two or three training sessions like this, make it more challenging by backing up slowly, quickly, or by making

Guaranteed by the manufacturer to stop any dog of any size or weight from ever pulling again. It's like having power steering for your dog. Photo courtesy of Four Paws.

IF YOUR PUPPY BALKS

If your puppy balks, do not use the leash to drag him to you. This will cause him to dig his feet in and apply the brakes. Instead, kneel down, open your arms wide, and encourage him to you, "Hey, Sweetie, here! Good boy!" When he dashes to your lap, praise him and tell him what a wonderful puppy he is. Then try the exercise again.

turns. If he gets confused or balks, make it simple until he's willingly following you again.

INTRODUCING THE CAR

Many puppies are afraid of the car, because a ride in the car was the first strange thing to happen to them when they were taken from their mother and littermates. The car also takes them to the veterinarian's office, another strange place where someone in a white coat pokes them, prods them, and gives them shots. You don't want this fear of the car to grab hold, though—you want your puppy to understand that riding in the car is something fun to do.

Start by lifting your puppy into the car and handing him a treat. As soon as he finishes the treat, lift him down and walk

springer spaniel

For some dogs, the car can be a frightening place. If you acclimate your Springer to the car at an early age, he will soon look forward to traveling with you.

away. Repeat this simple exercise several times a day for a few days. Then lift him into the car, give him a treat, let him eat it, and let him explore the car for a few minutes. After he has sniffed for a few minutes, give him another treat, let him eat it, then lift him down and walk away. Continue this training for a week or two, depending on how nervous your puppy is in the car.

When your puppy is expecting a treat in the car, put his crate in the car and strap it down securely. Put your puppy in his crate, give him a treat, and then start the car's engine. Back down the driveway and then back up to the house. Stop the engine, give your puppy a treat, and let him out of his crate and the car.

The next time, drive down the street and then back. Then go around the block. Increase the distances and times of the drives very gradually. You want your puppy to expect good things in the car, not scary things. Your Springer puppy will have a lifetime of car rides ahead of him, and life

Your local pet shop sells excellent grooming supplies, which can sometimes be purchased in affordable combination packages. Photo courtesy of Wahl, USA.

will be much nicer if he enjoys the rides.

SOCIAL HANDLING

Your Springer puppy cannot care for himself. You must be able to brush and comb him, bathe him, check his feet for cuts and scrapes, and clean his ears. Your Springer puppy doesn't understand why you need to do these annoying things to him, and he may struggle when you try to care for him. This social handling exercise will help teach your puppy to accept your care:

END ON A HIGH NOTE

Always end these (and all) training sessions on a high note. If your Springer puppy is worried, scared, and confused, help him do something right and then end the training session with that praise. Never end the training session at a negative point in the training or it will affect his outlook toward training later.

Photo by Isabelle Francais

It's a good idea to put your puppy in a place where he will feel secure and safe, preferably in your room. If he feels lonely or scared, he is more apt to get into trouble.

checking for cuts, scratches, lumps, bumps, bruises, fleas, ticks, or any other problems that need to be taken care of.

Once your puppy has learned to enjoy this handling you can clean his ears, wash out his eyes, trim his toenails, or do anything else that needs doing during the massage. This is also an excellent time to introduce your Springer to grooming, something he should learn to enjoy since it will be a regular part of his life. Start brushing and combing him while he's in this position, and praise him when he relaxes.

Sit down on the floor with your puppy and have him lie down between your legs. He can lie on his back or on his side; let him get comfortable. Start by giving him a slow, easy tummy rub. The idea here is to relax him—if your movements are fast and vigorous, you'll make him want to play. Keep it slow and gentle. If he starts to struggle, tell him calmly, "Easy. Be still." Restrain him gently if you need to do so.

When your puppy is relaxed, start giving him a massage. Start at his neck and ears, gently rubbing all around the base of each ear and working down the neck to the shoulders. Continue over his body, gently massaging it while at the same time

RELAX!

You can also use the social handling exercise to relax your puppy when he's over-stimulated. If you let him in from the backyard and he's full of Springer energy, don't chase him down or try to correct him. Instead, sit down on the floor and invite him to join you. (Use a treat to get him to come to you if you need some extra incentive.) Once he's come to you, lay him down and begin the massage. He will relax and calm down, and in the process, you are giving him the attention he needs from you.

The Basic
OBEDIENCE
Commands

Many dog owners are embarrassed to admit their dog needs training. "He does everything I ask," they say. Yet when they are asked specific questions about behavior, their answer changes, "Oh, he jumps on guests once in a while, and he does raid the trash can—but only when there is good trash in it—and yes, once he chewed on the corner of the sofa...hmm, maybe he *could* use a *little* training!"

Dog owners benefit from training, too. During training, you learn how to teach your Springer and how to motivate him to be good so that you can encourage good behavior. You also learn how to prevent problem behavior from happening and how to correct the inevitable mistakes.

Training helps your dog to be obedient and well behaved. During training, dog owners learn how to motivate their Springer to want to behave correctly.

Photo by Vince Serbin

springer spaniel

This Springer gets a little help in learning how to sit on command. Show your dog what you want him to do and give him a verbal command to correspond with the action.

THE TEACHING PROCESS

Teaching your dog what you want him to know is a process. This process begins with teaching him that certain words have meanings and that you would like him to follow your directions. Your English Springer Spaniel is very intelligent, but he doesn't understand why you want him to do these things— after all, why should he sit? He doesn't know why sitting is so important to you. Therefore, teaching him must also include motivating your dog to *want* to do the things you ask him to do.

Show Your Dog

First of all, you want to show your dog what it is you want him to do and that there is a word—a human spoken sound—associated with that action or position. For example, when teaching him to sit, you can help him into position as you tell him "Sweetie, sit." Follow that with praise, "Good boy to sit!" even if you helped him into position.

You will follow a similar pattern when teaching your dog most new things. If you want him off the sofa, you can tell him, "Sweetie, off the furniture," as you take him by the collar and pull him off. When he's off the furniture, tell him, "Good boy to get off the furniture."

Treats can be used as a motivational tool in the training process. If your Springer is rewarded for his efforts, he will try harder and pay more attention to you.

Praise

Praise him every time he does something right even if you help him do it. Your Springer will pay more attention and try harder if he is praised for his efforts. However, don't praise him when it's undeserved. Springers are very intelligent dogs and will quickly figure this out. Instead, give enthusiastic praise when he makes an effort and does something right for you.

Correct

Do not correct your dog until he understands what it is you want him to do. After he understands, is willing to obey the command, and then chooses

not to do it, you can then correct him with a verbal correction, "Sweetie, no!" or a quick snap and release of the collar. Use *only* as much correction as is needed to get his attention and *no more*. With corrections, less is usually better as long as your dog is responding.

Your Timing

The timing of your praise, corrections, and interruptions is very important. Praise him *as* he is doing something right. Correct him *when* he makes the mistake. Interrupt him *as* he starts to stick his nose into the trash can. If your timing is slow, he may not understand what you are trying to teach him.

Be Fair

Springers resent corrections that are too harsh or unfair. They will show this resentment by refusing to work, by planting themselves and refusing to move, or by fighting back. Some Springers will even show signs of

want, but lavishly praise the actions you want to continue.

THE BASIC COMMANDS

Sit and Release

The sit is the foundation command for everything else your Springer will learn. When your Springer learns to sit still, he

The sit is the foundation for every other command your Springer will learn.

depression if a harsh training method continues.

Interruptions and corrections alone will not teach your Springer. They are used to stop—at that precise moment—undesirable behavior or actions. Your Springer learns much more when you reward good behavior. Stop the behavior you don't

learns to control himself and that there are consequences to his actions. This is a very big lesson.

The sit is also a good alternative action for problem behavior. Your Springer cannot both sit still and jump on you. Therefore, learning to sit still for praise can replace jumping up on people for attention. He can't

One of the two methods used to teach your dog the sit command involves treats. As your Springer watches the treat in your hand move toward his tail, he will gradually move into a sitting position.

his head goes up and back, his hips will go down. As he sits, praise him, "Good boy to sit!" and give him a treat. Pet him in the sitting position.

When you are ready for him to get up, tap him on the shoulder as you tell him, "Release!" Each exercise needs a beginning and an end. The sit command is the beginning, and the release command tells him he is done and can move now. If he doesn't get up on his own, use your hands on his collar to walk him forward.

knock his food bowl out of your hand if he's sitting still, waiting patiently for his dinner. You can fasten his leash to his collar more easily if he's sitting still. This is a practical, useful command!

There are two basic methods of teaching your Springer to sit. Some dogs do better with one technique than the other, so try both to see which is better for your Springer.

Hold your Springer's leash in your left hand, and have some treats in your right hand. Tell your Springer, "Sweetie, sit!" as you move your right hand (with the treats) from his nose over his head towards his tail. He will lift his head to watch your hand. As

USE INTERRUPTIONS

Interrupt incorrect behavior as you see it happen. If your dog is walking by the kitchen trash can and turns to sniff it, interrupt him, "Leave it alone!" If you tell him to sit and he does, but then starts to get up, interrupt him, "No! Sit." By interrupting him, you can stop incorrect behavior before or as it happens.

If your Springer is too excited by the treats to think (and some Springers are like that), put the treats away. Tell your Springer to sit as you place one hand under his chin on the front of the neck, sliding the other hand down his hips to tuck his back legs under. Gently shape him into a sit as you give him the command, "Sweetie, sit." Praise him and release him.

Have your Springer in a sitting position when teaching him the stay command. An open-palmed gesture along with a verbal command will indicate he should stay until you release him.

springer spaniel

SIT, PLEASE!

Once your Springer understands the sit command and is responding well, start having him sit for things that he wants. Have him sit before you hook his leash to his collar for a walk, give him a treat, give him his meals, or throw his ball.

By giving your Springer a tummy rub while he's in the down position, you are showing him that it can be relaxing and fun.

If your dog is wiggly as you try to teach this exercise, keep your hands on him. If he pops up, interrupt that action in a deep, firm tone of voice, "Be still!" When he responds and stops wiggling, praise him quietly and gently.

Down

The down exercise continues one of the lessons the sit command started, that of self-control. It is hard for many energetic, bouncy young Springers to control their own actions, but it is a lesson all must learn. Practicing the down exercise teaches your Springer to lie down and be still.

Start with your Springer in a sit. Rest one hand gently on his shoulder and have a treat in the other hand. Let him smell the treat and then tell him, "Sweetie, down," taking the treat straight down to the ground in front of his front paws. As he follows the treat down, use your hand on his shoulders to encourage him to lie down. Praise him, give him the treat, and then have him hold the position for a moment. Release him in the same way you did from the sit—pat him on the shoulder, tell him "Release!" and let him get up.

If your dog looks at the treat as you make the signal but doesn't follow the treat to the ground, simply scoop his front legs up and forward as you lay

ONE COMMAND

Don't keep repeating any command. The command is not, "Sit! Sit, sit, sit, please sit. SIT!!" If you give repeated commands for the sit, your Springer will assume that carries over to everything else. Tell him one time to sit, and then help him do it.

In order for the sit and down commands to be effective, your dog has to learn how to stay in those positions. This Springer practices staying while in the down.

him down. The rest of the exercise is the same.

As your Springer learns what the down command means, you can have him hold it for a few minutes longer before you release him, but do not step away from him yet. Stay next to him, and if he's wiggly, keep a hand on his shoulder to help him stay in position.

Once each day, have your Springer lie down, and then before you release him, roll him over for a tummy rub. He will enjoy the tummy rub, relax a little, and learn to enjoy the down position. This is especially important for young Springers who want to do anything *but* lie down and hold still.

BE FAIR

Make sure you make it very clear what you want your dog to do. Remember, something is either right or wrong to your dog—it's not partly right or partly wrong. Be fair with your commands, your praise, and your corrections.

Stay

When your Springer understands both the sit and down commands, you can introduce him to the stay exercise. You want to convey to your Springer that the word "stay" means "hold still." When able to hold the sit position for several minutes and the down for even longer.

Start by having your Springer sit. With the leash in your left hand, use the leash to put a slight bit of pressure backward (toward his tail) as

The stay command can be useful around the house, especially when you don't want your Springer jumping all over your guests or begging for food at the dinner table.

your dog is sitting and you tell him to stay, you want him to remain in the sitting position until you go back to him and release him. When you tell him to stay while he's lying down, you want him to remain lying down until you go back to him and release him from that position. Eventually, he will be you tell him, "Sweetie, stay." At the same time, use your right hand to give your dog a hand signal that will mean stay—an open-handed gesture with the palm toward your dog's face. Take one step away and at the same time, release the pressure on the leash.

If your dog moves or gets

up, tell him "No!" so that he knows he made a mistake, and put him back into position. Repeat the exercise. After a few seconds, go back to him and praise him. Don't let him move from position until you release him.

Use the same process to teach the stay in the down position.

With the stay commands, you always want to go back to your Springer to release him. Don't release him from a distance or call him to come from the stay. If you do either of these, your dog will be much less reliable on the stay—he will continue to get up from the stay because you will have taught him to do exactly that. When teaching the stay, you want your Springer to learn that stay means "Hold this position until I come back to you to release you."

As your Springer learns the stay command, you can *gradually* increase the time you ask him to hold it. However, if your dog is making a lot of mistakes and moving often, you are either asking him to hold it too long or he doesn't understand the command yet. In either case, go back and reteach the exercise from the beginning.

Increase your distance from your dog very gradually, too. Again, if your dog is making a lot of mistakes, you're moving away too quickly.

This Springer demonstrates the "watch me" exercise, which teaches your dog to ignore distractions and pay attention to you.

When your Springer understands the stay command but chooses not to do it, you need to let him know the command is not optional. Many young, wiggly Springers want to do anything except hold still. However, holding still is very important to Springer owners. Correct excess movement first with

Once your Springer can easily demonstrate one exercise, move onto another. It's a good idea to keep the training challenging and rewarding.

your voice, "No! Be still! Stay!" and if that doesn't stop the excess movement, use a verbal correction and a snap and release of the leash. When he does control himself, praise him enthusiastically.

Watch Me

The "watch me" exercise teaches your English Springer Spaniel to ignore distractions and pay attention to you. This is particularly useful when you're out in public and your dog is distracted by children playing or dogs barking behind a fence.

USING THE STAY COMMAND

You can use the stay command around the house. For example, in the evening while you're watching a favorite television show, have your Springer lie down at your feet while you sit on the sofa. Give him a toy to chew on and tell him, "Sweetie, stay." Have him do a down/stay when guests visit so he isn't jumping all over them. Have him lie down and stay while the family is eating so he isn't begging under the table. There are a lot of practical uses for the stay. Just look at your normal routine and see where this command can work for you.

Start by having your Springer sit in front of you. Have a treat in your right hand. Let him sniff the treat and then tell him, "Sweetie, watch me!" as you take the treat from his nose up to your chin. When his eyes follow the treat in your hand and he looks at your face, praise him, "Good boy to watch me!" and give him the treat. Then release him from the sit. Repeat it again exactly the same way two or three times, and then quit for that training session.

Because this is hard for young, bouncing Springers, practice it first at home when there are few distractions. Make sure your dog knows it well before you take him

The heel command means to have your Springer walk by your side and maintain that position. Your dog needs to be able to demonstrate all of the commands if he is going to compete in dog shows.

Photo by Isabelle Francais

springer spaniel

Training is a one-on-one process with your dog. It not only helps to strengthen the relationship between dog and owner, but it also builds confidence and understanding.

Have him sit in front of you, and tell him to watch you. As he watches you, take a few steps backward and ask him to follow you and watch you at the same time. Praise him when he does. Try it again. When he can follow you six or seven steps and watch you at the same time, make it more challenging—back up and turn to the left or right, or back up faster. Praise him when he continues to watch you!

Heel

You want your Springer to learn that "heel" means "Walk by my left side, with your neck and shoulders by my left leg, and maintain that position." Ideally, your Springer should maintain that position as you walk slowly, quickly, turn corners, or weave in and out through a crowd.

outside and try to practice it with distractions. However, once he knows it well inside, then you need to try it with distractions. Take him out in the front yard (on his leash, of course) and tell him to watch you. If he ignores you, take his chin in your left hand (the treat is in the right hand) and hold it so that he has to look at your face. Praise him even though you are helping him do it.

When he will watch you out front with some distractions, then move on to the next step.

To start, practice a "watch me" exercise to get your dog's attention on you. Back away from him and encourage him to watch you. When he does, simply turn your body as you are backing up so that your dog ends up on your left side, and continue walking. If you have done it correctly, it is one smooth movement, so you and your dog end up walking forward together with your dog on your left side.

Let's walk through it in slow motion. Sit your dog in front of you and do a "watch me." Back away from your dog and encourage him to follow you. When he's watching you, back up toward your left and as you are backing up, continue turning in that direction so you and your dog end up walking forward together. Your dog should end up on your left side with you on his right side.

If your dog starts to pull forward, simply back away from him and encourage him to follow you. If you need to do so, use the leash with a snap-and-release motion to make the dog follow you. Praise him when he does.

Don't hesitate to go back and forth—walking forward and then backing away—if you need to do so. In fact, sometimes this can be the best exercise you can do to get your dog's attention on you.

When your dog is walking nicely with you and paying attention to you, you can start eliminating the backing away. Start the heel with your Springer sitting by your left side. Tell him, "Sweetie, watch me! Heel." Start walking. When he's walking nicely with you, praise him. However, if he

gets distracted or starts to pull, simply back away from him again.

Come

The come command is one of the most important commands your Springer needs to learn. Not only is the come command important around the house in your daily routine, but it could also be a lifesaver

Using treats, you can get your dog to realize that coming to you will result in a reward.

someday, especially if your dog should decide to dash toward the street when a car is coming. Because the come command is so important, you will use two different techniques to teach your dog to come to you when you call him.

Come with a Treat

The first technique will use a sound stimulus and a treat to teach your Springer to come when you call him. Take a small plastic container (such as a margarine tub) and put a handful of dry dog food in it. Put the lid on and shake it to make a nice rattling sound.

Have the shaker in one hand and some good dog treats in the other. Shake the container, and as your Springer looks at it and you, ask him, "Sweetie, cookie?" Use whatever word he already knows means treat. When you say "cookie," pop a treat in his mouth. Do it again. Shake, shake, say "Sweetie, cookie?" and pop a treat in his mouth.

The sound of the container, your verbal question, and the treat are all becoming associated in his mind. He is learning that the sound of the container equals the treat—an important lesson. Do this several times a day for several days.

Then, with him sitting in front of you, replace the word "cookie" with the word "come." Shake the container, say "Sweetie, come!" and pop a

USING A SOUND STIMULUS

Do you remember those silent dog whistles that used to be advertised in comic books? There was nothing magical about those whistles, except that they were so high-pitched, dogs could hear them but people couldn't. The container we're using for teaching the come works on the same principle that the silent dog whistle used; it's a sound stimulus you can use to get the dog's attention so that you can teach him. By teaching him to pay attention to the sound of the shaker, and by teaching him that the sound of the shaker means he's going to get a treat, we can make coming when called that much more exciting. Your dog will be more likely to come to you (especially when there are distractions) if he's excited about it.

treat in his mouth. You are rewarding him even though he didn't actually come to you— he was still sitting in front of you. However, you are teaching him that the sound of the shaker now equals the word "come," and he still gets the treat. Another important lesson. Practice this several times a day for several days.

When your Springer is happy to hear the shaker and is drooling to get a treat, start calling him across the room. Shake the container as you say, "Sweetie, come!" When he dashes to you, continue to give him a treat as you praise him, "Good boy to come!" Practice this up and down the hallway, inside and outside, and across the backyard. Make it fun, keeping up with the treats and the verbal praise.

When your Springer learns the sit command, he learns how to control himself and that there are consequences to his actions.

Photo by Isabelle Francais

DON'T WORRY

Some people have reservations about this technique because they are worried the dog will not come to them when they don't have a treat. First of all, you will use two different techniques to teach the come command and only one technique uses the treats. Second, even with this technique, you will eventually stop using treats. However, by using this technique when first introducing the come command, you can produce such a strong, reliable response, that it's worth all of your efforts.

The Come with a Long Line

The second method to teach your dog to come uses a long leash or a length of clothesline rope. Because Springers are athletic and fast, use a line at least 30 feet in length. Fasten the line to your Springer's collar and then let him go play. When he is distracted by something, call him to come, "Sweetie, come!" If he responds and comes right away, praise him.

If he doesn't respond right away, do *not* call him again. Pick up the line, back away from him, and use the line to make him come to you. Do not give him a verbal correction at this time—he may associate the verbal correction with coming to you. Instead, simply make him come to you even if you have to drag him in with the line.

Let him go again and repeat

DON'T USE THE COME COMMAND TO PUNISH

Never call your dog to come and then punish him for something he did earlier. Not only is the late punishment ineffective (it always is), but that unfair punishment will teach your dog to avoid you when you call him. Keep the come command positive all the time.

the entire exercise. Make sure you always praise him when he does decide to come to you. If he is really distracted, use the shaker and treats along with the long line, especially in the early stages

The long line can be used as an aid in helping your Springer learn the come command. Because Springers are very athletic and quick, use a line at least 30 feet in length.

of the training. You can always wean him from the treats later—right now you want to make the come command work.

Don't allow your Springer to have freedom off the leash until he is grown up enough to handle the responsibility and is very well trained. Many dog owners let their dog off leash much too soon, and the dogs learn bad habits their owners wish they hadn't learned. Each time your dog is allowed to ignore you or run away from you, it reinforces the fact that he can. Instead, let him run around and play while dragging the long line. That way you can always regain control when you need it.

USE IT OR LOSE IT

The best way to make this training work for you and your Springer is to use it. Training is not just for training sessions—instead, training is for your daily life. Incorporate it into your daily routine. Have your Springer sit before you feed him. Have him lie down and stay while you eat. Have him sit and stay at the gate while you take the trash cans out. Have him do a down/stay when guests come over. Use these commands as part of your life. They will work much better that way.

All About
F O R M A L
Training

Formal dog training is much more than the traditional sit, down, stay, and come commands. Dog training means teaching your English Springer Spaniel that he's living in your house, not his. It means you can set some rules and expect him to follow them. It will not turn your Springer into a robot—instead it will teach your Springer to look at you in a new light. Training will cause you to look at him differently, too. Training is not something you do *to* your Springer; it's something you do together.

TRAINING METHODS

If you were to talk to 100 dog trainers (someone who trains dogs) or dog obedience instructors (someone who teaches the dog owner how to teach his dog) and ask them how they train, you would get 100 different answers. Any trainer or instructor who has been in the business for any period of time is going to work out a method or technique that works best for her. Each method will be based on the trainer's personality, teaching techniques, experience, and philosophy on dogs and dog training. Any given method may work wonderfully for one trainer but fail terribly for another.

Because there are so many different techniques, styles, and methods, choosing a particular instructor may be difficult. It is important to understand some

Once your Springer has completed basic obedience training, including all of the commands, you can continue on to a more advanced program.

Photo by Isabelle Francais

There are many different techniques used in formal training. Talk to several instructors or trainers to find out which method will work best for you and your dog.

of the different methods so that you can make a reasonable decision.

Compulsive Training

Compulsive training is a method of training that forces the dog to behave. This is usually a correction-based training style, sometimes with forceful corrections. This training is usually used with law enforcement and military dogs and can be quite effective with hard-driving, strong-willed dogs. Many pet dog owners do not like this style of training, feeling it is too rough.

Inducive Training

This training is exactly the opposite of compulsive training. Instead of being forced to do something, the dog is induced or motivated toward proper behavior. Depending on the instructor, there are few or no corrections used. This training works very well for most puppies, for softer dogs, and sometimes for owners who dislike corrections of any kind.

Unfortunately, this is not always the right technique for Springers. Many Springers will take advantage of the lack of corrections or discipline. Some very intelligent, dominant-personality dogs (including some Springers) look upon the lack of discipline as weakness on your part and will then set their own rules, which, unfortunately, may not be the rules you wish them to abide by.

Somewhere in the Middle

The majority of trainers and instructors use a training method that is somewhere in between both of these techniques. An inducive method is used when possible, while corrections are used when needed. Obviously, the range can be vast, with some trainers leaning toward more corrections while others use as few as possible.

Group Classes or Private Lessons?

There are benefits and drawbacks to both group classes and private lessons. In group classes, the dog must learn to behave around other distractions, specifically the other dogs and people in class. Since the world is made up of lots of things capable of distracting your Springer, this can work very well. In addition, a group class can work like group therapy for dog owners. The owners can share triumphs and mishaps and can encourage and support one another. Many friendships have begun in group training classes.

The drawback to group classes is that for some dogs the distractions of a group class are too much. Some dogs simply cannot concentrate at all, especially in the beginning of training. For these dogs, a few private lessons may help enough so that the dog can join a group class later. Dogs with severe behavior problems—especially aggression—should bypass group classes for obvious reasons.

Private lessons—one-on-one training with the owner,

Photo by Isabelle Francais

Compulsive training forces a dog to behave; inducive training motivates the dog toward proper behavior. The majority of trainers use a technique that falls somewhere between these two methods.

dog, and instructor—are also good for people with a very busy schedule who may otherwise not be able to do any training at all.

Puppy Class

Puppy or kindergarten classes are for puppies older than 10 weeks of age but not over 16 weeks. These classes are usually half obedience training and half socialization, because for puppies, both of these subjects are very important.

The puppy's owner also learns how to prevent problem behaviors from occurring and how to establish household rules.

Basic Obedience Class

This class is for puppies who have graduated from a puppy class, for puppies over four months of age that haven't attended a puppy class, or for adult dogs. In this class, the dogs and their owners work on basic obedience commands such as sit, down, stay, come, and heel. Most instructors also spend time discussing problem prevention and problem

GOALS FOR YOUR SPRINGER

What do you want training to accomplish? Do you want your Springer to be calm and well-behaved around family members? Do you want him to behave himself out in public? Would you like to participate in dog activities and sports? There are an unlimited number of things you can do with your Springer—it's up to you to decide what you would like to do. Then you can find a training program to help you achieve those goals. As you start training, talk to your trainer about them so she can guide you in the right direction.

One of the benefits to a group class is that your dog learns how to behave around other distractions, specifically the other dogs and people in class.

springer spaniel

solving, especially the common problems like jumping on people, barking, digging, and chewing.

Dog Sports Training

Some instructors offer training for one or more of the various dog activities or sports. There are classes to prepare you for competition in obedience trials, conformation dog shows, flyball, agility, or field trials. Other trainers may offer training for noncompetitive activities such as therapy dog work.

FINDING AN INSTRUCTOR OR TRAINER

When trying to find an instructor or trainer, word-of-mouth referrals are probably the best place to start. Although anyone can place an advertisement in the newspaper or yellow pages, the ad itself is no guarantee of quality or expertise. However, happy customers will demonstrate their experience with well-behaved dogs and will be glad to tell you where they received instruction.

You can do many different things with your Springer. First, establish goals for your dog and then find an instructor that can help you achieve them.

Photo by Isabelle Francais

Photo by Isabelle Francais

If your Springer has trouble learning the commands, you can enroll him in a basic obedience class. You get a chance to work with your dog, while at the same time receive professional help.

ADVANCED TRAINING

Advanced training classes vary depending on the instructor. Some offer classes to teach you to control your dog off leash, some emphasize dog sports, and others may simply continue basic training skills. Ask the instructor what she offers.

Have you admired a neighbor's well-behaved dog? Ask where they went for training. Call your veterinarian, local pet store, or groomer, and ask who they recommend. Make notes about each referral. What did people like about this trainer? What did they dislike?

Once you have a list of referrals, start calling the instructors and ask each one a few questions. How long has she been teaching classes? You will want someone with experience, of course, so that she can handle the various situations that may arise. However, experience alone is not the only qualification. Some people who have been trainers for years are still teaching exactly the same way they did many years ago and have never learned anything new.

Ask the instructor about

Photo by Isabelle Francais

This energetic Springer shows off his agility skills while sailing through the tire jump.

English Springer Spaniels. What does she think of the breed? Ideally, she should be knowledgeable about the breed, what makes them tick, and how to train them. She should also be aware of rage syndrome—ask her if she has dealt with it and how often. Don't be put off if she says she refers dogs suspected of having rage syndrome to a behaviorist or a veterinarian; actually, that's good advice for a trainer, especially if she teaches group classes. A dog with rage syndrome probably needs more help than a group class can offer.

Ask the instructor to explain her training methods. Does this sound like something you would be comfortable with? Ask if there are alternative methods used. Not every dog will respond the same way, and every instructor should have a backup plan.

Does the instructor belong to any professional organizations? The National Association of Dog Obedience Instructors (NADOI) and the Association of Pet Dog Trainers (APDT) are two of the more prominent groups. Both of these organizations publish regular newsletters to share information, techniques, new developments, and more. Instructors belonging to organizations such as these are more likely to be up-to-date on training techniques, styles, and so forth, as well as information about specific dog breeds.

Make sure, too, that the instructor will be able to help you achieve your goals. For example, if you want to compete in obedience trials, the instructor should have experience in that field and knowledge of the rules and regulations of that competition.

After talking to several trainers or instructors, ask if you can watch their training or classes. If they say no, cross them off your list. There should be no reason why you cannot attend one class to see if you will be comfortable with this instructor and her style of teaching. As you watch the class, see how the trainer handles students' dogs. Would you let her handle your dog? How does she relate to the students? Are they relaxed? Do

they look like they're having a good time? Are they paying attention to her?

After talking to the instructor or trainer and after watching a class, you should know which class you want to attend. If you're still undecided,

Training helps to build a stronger, more secure relationship between you and your dog.

call the instructors back and ask a few more questions. After all, you are hiring them to provide a service, and you must be comfortable with your decision.

BUILDING A RELATIONSHIP

Training helps build a relationship between you and your dog. This relationship is built on mutual trust, affection, and respect. Training can help your dog become your best friend—a well-behaved companion that is a joy to spend time with and that won't send your blood pressure sky-high!

Problem
PREVENTION
and Solving

Springers are an intelligent, easily trained breed, so many Springer owners are flabbergasted when they find their beloved dog has chewed up their new leather shoes or chased the family cat to the top of the china hutch. Springers can also be barkers, which can cause untold trouble with the neighbors. Springers can also jump on people, raid the trash can, or uproot the garden. This is not to say Springers are horrible dogs. On the contrary, Springers are wonderful dogs. However, every dog can exhibit some problem behavior with many possible causes, and solving it isn't always easy.

Many of the behaviors that dog owners consider problems—barking, digging, chewing, jumping up on people, and so on—are very natural behaviors to your Springer. Springers *like* to jump; that's where the breed's name came from. Dogs dig because the dirt

Training can play a big part in controlling problem behavior. A firm approach shows your Springer that you are in charge and that he must adhere to your rules and regulations.

springer spaniel

71

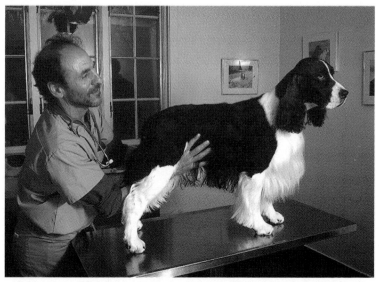

If your Springer's behavior suddenly changes, it's possible that health problems could be the cause. Take him to the vet before you start any training.

smells good or because there's a gopher in the yard. Dogs bark to verbalize something, just as people talk. However, most problem behaviors can be addressed and either prevented, controlled, or in some cases, stopped entirely.

TRAINING

Training can play a big part in controlling problem behavior. A fair, upbeat, yet firm training program teaches your dog that you are in charge and that he is below you in the family pack. The training should also reinforce his concept of you as a kind, calm, caring leader. In addition, your training skills give you the ability to teach your dog what is acceptable and what is not.

WHAT YOU CAN DO

Health Problems

Some experts feel that 20 percent of all common behavior problems are caused by health problems. A bladder infection or gastrointestinal upset commonly causes housetraining accidents. Thyroid problems can cause a behavior change, as can medications, hyperactivity, hormone imbalances, and a variety of other health problems.

If your dog's behavior changes, make an appointment with your veterinarian. Tell your vet why you are bringing the dog in; don't just ask for an exam. Explain that your Springer has changed his behavior, tell what the behavior is, and ask if the vet could examine the dog for any physical problems that could lead to that type of behavior.

Don't automatically assume your dog is healthy. If a health problem is causing the behavior change, training or behavior modification won't make it better. Before beginning any training, talk to your veterinarian. Once health problems are ruled out, you can start working on the problem itself.

It is vitally important that you talk to your veterinarian right away if your Springer shows sudden or unexplained signs of aggression. Rage syndrome isn't common. However, it needs to be identified, if at all possible, *before* your dog hurts someone.

Owners of Springers with rage syndrome mention one common symptom other than unexplained aggression: During the fits of rage, their dogs had a blank look in their eyes, a glassy stare—almost as if the dog wasn't actually in contact with the world. If your dog shows unexplained or sudden aggression in conjunction with a strange look in his eyes, contact your veterinarian right away.

Nutrition

Nutrition can play a part in causing or solving behavior problems. If your dog is eating a poor-quality food or if he cannot digest the food he is being fed, his body may be missing some vital nutrients. If your Springer is

Proper nutrition is imperative to your dog's health. Veterinarians recommend elevated feeders to help reduce stress on your dog's neck and back muscles. The raised platform also provides better digestion while reducing bloating and gas. Photo courtesy of Pet Zone Products, Ltd.

Foods containing high levels of linoleic acid will help to maintain a healthy skin and shiny coat in your dog; foods containing high levels of digestible proteins are also desirable. Photo courtesy of Nutro Products, Inc.

chewing on rocks or wood, chewing the stucco off the side of your house, or grazing on the plants in your garden, he may have a nutritional deficiency of some kind.

Some dogs develop a type of hyperactivity when fed a high-calorie, high-fat dog food. Other dogs have food allergies that may show up as behavior problems.

If you have any questions about the food your dog is eating, talk to your veterinarian.

Play

Play is different from exercise, although exercise can be play. The key to play is laughter. Researchers know that laughter is wonderful medicine—it makes you feel better about the world around you. Laughter and play have a special place in your relationship with your Springer. Springers can be very silly, and you should take advantage of that—laugh at your dog and with him. Play games that will make you laugh. Play is also a great stress reliever. Make time for play when you are having a hard time at work. Play with your Springer after your training sessions.

Sometimes dogs get into trouble intentionally because they feel ignored. To these dogs, any attention—even corrections or yelling—is better teach him tricks, and take him on muddy treks through the woods. It doesn't matter what you do, as long as you and your dog do something fun together.

Prevent Problems From Happening

Because so many of the things we consider problems are natural behaviors to your

Provide your Springer with various toys to keep him occupied when you can't be the center of his attention. This will keep his jaw exercised and keep him out of trouble.

than no attention at all. If you regularly take time to play with your dog, you can avoid some of these situations.

Springers love to play and will continue playing long into adulthood when many other breeds no longer have any desire to play. This trait is what makes the breed so appealing to many people. Take advantage of it by playing with your dog. Play hide-and-seek,

EXERCISE

Exercise is just as important for your Springer as it is for you. Exercise works the body, uses up excess energy, relieves stress, and clears the mind. How much exercise is needed depends on your dog and your normal routine. A fast-paced walk might be enough for an older Springer, but a young, healthy Springer might need a good run or energetic game of fetch.

Control your Springer's urge to jump up by emphasizing the sit command. Help your dog understand that he doesn't have to jump to receive affection or treats.

Part of preventing problems from occurring also requires that you limit your dog's freedom. A young puppy or untrained dog should never have unsupervised free run of the house—there is simply too much he can get into. Instead, keep him close to you and close off rooms. If you can't watch him, put him into his run or out in the backyard.

DEALING WITH SPECIFIC PROBLEMS

Jumping on People

Just about every Springer owner, at one time or another, has to deal with their dog jumping up on people. That's just the way the breed is. And unfortunately, Springers don't simply jump up, they jump high. Some people joke that's how the breed got their name—they have springs in their paws.

You can, however, control the jumping by emphasizing the sit command. If your Springer is sitting, he can't jump up. By teaching him to sit for petting, praise, treats, and his meals, you can teach him that sitting is important and that everything he wants will happen only when he sits.

Use the leash as much as you can to teach your Springer to sit. When you come home from

Springer, you need to prevent as many of them from happening as you reasonably can. Put the trash cans away so that he never discovers that the kitchen trash can is full of good-tasting surprises. Make sure the kids put their toys away so that your Springer can't chew them to pieces. It's much easier to prevent a problem from happening than it is to break a bad habit later.

Preventing a problem from happening might require that you fence off the garden, build higher shelves in the garage, or maybe even build your Springer a dog run.

A DOG RUN

A dog run is not a dog prison. Instead, it is a safe place for him to stay while he's unsupervised. In his dog run, he should have protection from the sun and weather, unspillable water, and a few toys. Don't put him in his run as punishment, and never scold him there. Instead, give him a treat or a toy when you put him in his run. Leave a radio playing quiet, gentle music in a nearby window.

work, don't greet your dog until you have a leash and collar in hand. As your dog greets you, slip the leash over his head. Then you can help him sit. If he tries to jump, give him a snap and release of the leash and a verbal correction, "No jump! Sit!" Of course, as with all of your training, praise him when he sits.

When you are out in public, make sure your Springer sits before any of your neighbors or friends pet him. Again, use your leash. If he won't sit still, don't let anyone pet him even if you have to explain your actions, "I'm sorry, but I'm trying to teach him manners and he must sit before he gets any petting."

The key to correcting jumping up is to make sure the bad behavior is not rewarded. If someone pets your Springer when he jumps up, that jumping has been rewarded. However, when he learns that he only gets attention when he's sitting, sitting will be much more attractive to him.

Digging

If your backyard looks like a military artillery range, you need to concentrate first on preventing this problem from occurring. If you come home from work to find new holes in the lawn or garden, don't correct the dog then. He probably dug the holes when you first left in the morning, and a correction ten hours later won't work.

Instead, build him a dog run and leave him there during the

A dog run is a great way for your Springer to get exercise and release excess energy when you can't watch him.

Photo by Isabelle Francais

If your Springer has the urge to dash through gates and doors before you, simply enforce the sit command. By teaching him to sit and wait for permission, you will be eliminating the problem.

playtime every day to use up his energy, stimulate his mind, and give him time with you. Most importantly, don't let a dog who likes to dig watch you garden. If you do, he may come to you later with all of those bulbs you planted earlier!

The Barker

Springers can be problem barkers, unfortunately. Springers bark when they are happy, when they want to play, when playing together or with people, and when someone is approaching the house. A Springer left alone for many hours each day may find that barking gets him attention, especially if your neighbors yell at him.

Start teaching him to be quiet when you're at home with him. When your Springer starts barking, tell him, "Quiet!" When he stops, praise him. When he understands what you want, go for a short walk outside, leaving him home. Listen, and when you hear him start barking, come back and correct him. After a few corrections, when he seems to understand, ask a neighbor to help you. Go outside and ask your neighbor to come out to talk. Have the kids outside playing. When your dog barks because he's feeling left out, go back and correct him. Repeat

day. If you fence off one side of your yard alongside your house, you might be able to give him a run that is 6 feet wide by 20 feet long. That's a great run. Let him trash this section to his heart's content—that's *his* yard.

Then when you are home and can supervise him, you can let him have free run of the rest of your yard. When he starts to get into trouble, you can use your voice to interrupt him, "Hey! What are you doing? Get out of the garden!"

The destructive dog also needs exercise, training, and

as often as you need to until he understands.

You can reduce your dog's emotional need to bark if you make coming home and leaving home quiet and low-keyed. When you leave the house, don't give him hugs and don't tell him repeatedly to be a good dog—that simply makes your leaving more emotional. Instead, give him attention an hour or two prior to your leaving, and when it's time for you to go, just go. When you come home, ignore your dog for a few minutes. Then whisper hello to him. Your Springer's hearing is very good, but to hear your whispers he is going to have to be quiet and still.

EXTRA HELP

Problem barkers may need extra help, especially if your neighbors are complaining. There are anti-bark collars on the market, and several are very humane and effective. All are triggered by the dog's barking and administer a correction to the dog. Some collars make a high-pitched sound, one squirts a whiff of citronella, and others administer a shock. I do not recommend the shock collars for most Springers, because many will panic at this type of correction. However, the first two types of collar are quite effective for many dogs.

You can also distract your dog when you leave. Take a brown paper lunch bag and put a couple of treats in it—maybe a dog biscuit, a piece of carrot, and a slice of apple. Roll the top over to close it, and rip a very tiny hole in the side to give your dog encouragement to get the treats. As you walk out the door or gate, hand the bag to your dog. He will be so busy figuring out where the treats are and how to get them, he'll forget you are leaving.

Dashing Through Doors and Gates

This is actually one of the easier behavior problems to solve. Teach your Springer to sit at all doors and gates, then hold that sit until you give him permission to go through or to get up after you have gone through. By teaching him to sit and wait for permission, you will eliminate the problem.

Start with your dog on the leash. Walk him up to a door. Have him sit, tell him to stay, and then open the door in front of him. If he dashes through, use the leash to correct him (snap and release) as you give him a verbal correction, "No! Stay!" Take him back to his original position and do it again. When he will hold it at this door, go

RUNNING FREE

If your Springer does make it out through a door or gate, don't chase him. The more you chase, the better the game as far as he's concerned. Instead, go get your shaker for training the come command. Shake it, say "Sweetie, do you want a cookie? Come!" When he comes back to you, you must praise him for coming even though you may want to wring his neck for dashing through the door. Don't correct him—a correction will make him avoid you even more the next time it happens.

to another door or gate and repeat the training procedure.

When he will wait (while on the leash) at all doors and gates, take his leash off and hook up his long line. Fasten one end of the long line to a piece of heavy furniture. Walk him up to the door and tell him to sit and stay. Drop the long line to the ground. With your hands empty, open the door and stand aside. Because your hands are empty (meaning you aren't holding the leash), your Springer may decide to dash. If he does, the long line will stop him, or you can step on the line. Give him a verbal correction, too, "No! I said stay!" and bring him back to where he started. Repeat the training session here and at all other doors and gates.

Other Problems?

Many behavior problems can be solved or at least controlled using similar techniques. Try to figure out why your Springer is doing what he's doing (from his point of view, not yours). What can you do to prevent the problem from happening? What can you do to teach your dog not to do it? Remember, as with all of your training, a correction alone will not change the behavior. You must also teach your dog what he can do. If you still have some problems, or if your dog is showing aggressive tendencies, contact your local dog trainer or behaviorist for some help.

Adorable faces like these can make leaving difficult, but don't get too emotional with your puppy when it's time for you to leave the house. This will reduce your Springer's need to bark or whine until you return.

Photo by Isabelle Francais

Advanced
TRAINING
and Dog Sports

If you and your Springer enjoy training, you may want to continue on with more advanced training. Hand signals and off-leash training are both fun and useful. In addition, a lot of the dog sports are fun and could be a great challenge to your training abilities.

HAND SIGNALS

When you start teaching hand signals, use a treat in your hand to get your Springer's attention. Use the verbal command he already knows to help him understand what you are trying to tell him. As he responds, decrease the verbal command to a whisper and emphasize the hand signal.

The difficult part about teaching hand signals is that in the beginning, your dog may not understand that these movements of your hand and arm have any significance. After all, people "talk" with their hands all the time—hands are always moving and waving. Dogs learn early to ignore hand and arm movements. Therefore, to make hand signals work, your Springer needs to watch you. A good treat in the hand making the movement can help.

USING HAND SIGNALS

Dog owners often think of hand signals as something that only really advanced dogs can respond to, and that is partly correct. It does take some training. However, hand signals are useful for all dog owners. For example, if your dog responds to hand signals, you can give him the signal to go lie down while you're talking on the telephone, and you won't have to interrupt your conversation to do so.

Hand signals are an important part of your Springer's learning process. This Springer and his owner demonstrate the signal for "down."

You want to be clear and concise when training your dog to respond to your commands.

Down

When you taught your Springer to lie down by taking the treat from his nose to the ground in front of his front paws, you were teaching him a hand signal. Granted, he was watching the treat in your hand, but he was also getting used to seeing your hand move. Therefore, switching him over from a verbal command to a hand-signal-only command should be easy.

Have your dog sit in front of you. Verbally, tell him, "Down" as you give him the hand signal for down (with a treat in your hand), just as you did when you were originally teaching it. When he lies down, praise him and then release him. Practice this a few times.

Now give him the signal to go down (with a treat in your hand), but do not give a verbal command. If he lies down, praise him, give him the treat, and release him. If he does not go down, give the leash a slight snap and release down toward the ground—not hard, but just enough to let him know, "Hey! Pay attention!" When he goes down, praise and release him.

When he can reliably follow the signal with no verbal command, make it more challenging. Signal him to lie down when you are across the room from him, while you're talking to someone, and when there are some distractions around him. Remember to praise him enthusiastically when he goes down on the signal.

Sit

If you were able to teach your Springer to sit using the treat above his nose, you were teaching him to sit using a hand signal. If you had to teach him by shaping him into a sit, you can still teach him a signal.

With your Springer on his leash, hold the leash in your left hand and a treat in your right hand. Stand in front of your Springer and take the treat from his nose upward. At the same time, whisper "Sit." When he sits, praise and release him. Try it again. When he is watching your hand and sitting reliably, stop whispering the command and let him follow the signal. If he doesn't sit, jiggle the leash and collar to remind him that something is expected. Again, when he sits, praise him.

Stay

When you taught the stay command, you used a hand signal: the open-palmed gesture toward your Springer's face. This signal is so obvious that your dog will probably do it without any additional training. Have your dog sit or lie down, and tell him to stay using only

Photo by Karen Taylor

This obedient Springer demonstrates the down/stay command.

the hand signal. Did he hold it? If he did, go back to him and praise him. If he didn't, use the leash to correct him (snap and release) and try it again.

Come

You want the signal for the come command to be a very broad, easily seen signal, one that your dog can recognize even if he's distracted by something. Therefore, this signal will be a wide swing of the right arm, starting with your arm held straight out to your side from the shoulder, horizontal to the ground. The motion will be

Photo by Isabelle Francais

Taking your Springer off leash can be a risk if he is not well trained. Before you let him roam freely, make sure that he willingly obeys your commands.

to bring the hand to your chest following a wide wave, as if you were reaching out to get your dog and bring him to you.

Start teaching the signal by having the shaker you used to teach the come command in your right hand as you start the signal. Shake it slightly, just to get your dog's attention, and

then complete the signal. Praise your dog when he responds and comes to you.

If he doesn't respond right away, start the signal again, and this time tell him verbally to come as you make the signal and shake the shaker. Again, praise him when he comes. Gradually eliminate the verbal command, and when your Springer is responding well, stop using the shaker.

OFF-LEASH CONTROL

One of the biggest mistakes many dog owners make is to take the dog off the leash too soon. When you take your dog off the leash, you have very little control—only your previous training can control your dog. If you take your dog off leash before you have established enough control or before your dog is mentally mature enough to accept that control, you are setting yourself up for disaster.

Springers are smart, curious dogs, and they love to check out new things, especially new smells. A rabbit is made to chase as far as Springers are concerned, and so is a butterfly or bird. More than one Springer has been so involved in his exploring that he's forgotten to pay attention to his owner's commands.

Before your Springer is to be allowed off his leash (outside of a fenced area or your backyard) you need to make sure your Springer's training is sound. He should be responding reliably and well to all of the basic commands.

Your Springer must also be mentally mature, which for some Springers might mean two, two-and-a-half, or even three years of age. He should be past the challenging teenage stage of development. Never take a young adolescent off leash outside of a fenced-in area; that is asking for a problem.

Come on a Long Line

The long line (or leash) was introduced earlier in the section on teaching the come command. It is also a good training technique for preparing your dog for off-leash control. Review that section and practice the come on the long line until you are comfortable your dog understands the come command from 20 to 30 feet away (the length of the long line) and will do it reliably.

Now, take him out to play in a different place that is still free from danger—a schoolyard is good. Let your Springer drag his long line behind him as he sniffs and explores. When he's distracted and not paying attention to you, call him to come. If he responds right away, praise him enthusiastically, telling him what a smart, wonderful dog he is.

Springers are very active and athletic dogs. It's important that you try as many different activities with your dog to keep him occupied and interested.

If he doesn't respond right away, step on the end of the long line, pick it up, and back away from him, calling him again as you use the long line to make him come to you. Don't beg him to come to you or repeat the come command over and over. Simply use the line to make him do it. This is not an optional command.

Heel

Most places require that dogs in public be leashed. However, teaching your Springer to heel without a leash is a good exercise. Not only is it a part of obedience competition (for people interested in that sport), but it's a good practical command, too. What would happen if your dog's leash or collar broke when you were out for a walk?

Accidents happen, but if your dog has already been trained to heel off leash, disaster will be averted.

To train for this, hook two leashes up to your dog's collar. Use your regular leash as well as a lightweight leash. Do a "watch me" exercise with treats and then tell your dog to heel. Practice a variety of things—walk slowly, quickly, turn corners, and perform figure eights. When your dog is paying attention well, reach down and unhook his regular leash, tossing it to the ground in front of him. If he bounces up, assuming he's free, correct him with the second leash, "Hey! I didn't release you!" and make him sit in the heel position. Hook his regular leash back up and repeat the exercise.

When he doesn't take advantage of the regular leash being taken off, tell him to heel and start practicing the heel. Do not use the second leash for minor correction, but save it for control. If he tries to dash away, pull from you, or otherwise break the heel exercise, use the second leash for correction and hook his regular leash back on again.

Repeat this, going back and forth between one leash and two, until he's not even thinking about whether his regular leash is on or not. You want him to work reliably without questioning the leash's control. For some Springers, this may take several weeks' worth of work.

When he is working reliably, put the second leash away. Take his regular leash, hook it up to his collar, and fold it up. Tuck it under his collar between his shoulder blades so that it is lying on his back. Practice his heel work. If he makes a mistake, grab the leash and collar as a handle and correct him. When the correction is over, take your hand off.

Expect and demand the same level of obedience off leash that you do on leash. Don't make excuses for off-leash work.

DOG SPORTS

Do you like training your Springer? If you and your Springer are having a good time, you may want to try one or more dog activities or sports. There are a lot of different things you can do with your dog—some competitive, some fun, and some good works. What you decide to do depends on you and your dog.

Conformation Competition

The American Kennel Club (AKC) and the United Kennel Club (UKC) both award conformation championships to purebred dogs. The requirements vary between the registries, but basically a championship is awarded when a purebred dog competes against other dogs of his breed and wins. The judge compares

Photo by Isabelle Francais

If you enjoy training your dog, there are many dog sports and competitions that you and your Springer can participate in.

each dog against a written standard for his breed and chooses the dog that most closely represents that standard of excellence.

This is a very simplistic explanation. However, if you feel your Springer is very handsome, you might want to go watch a few local dog shows.

Watch the Springers competing and talk to some of the Springer owners and handlers. Does your Springer still look like a good candidate? You will also want to do some reading about your breed and conformation competition and perhaps even attend a conformation class.

Obedience Competition

Obedience competition is a team sport involving you and

> **AGILITY**
> Agility is a fast-paced sport in which the dog must complete a series of obstacles correctly in a certain period of time, with the fastest time winning. Obstacles might include tunnels, hurdles, an elevated dog walk, and more. The AKC, the UKC, and the United States Dog Agility Association all sponsor agility competitions. Springers are very athletic, and some have been quite competitive in agility competitions.

your Springer. There are set exercises that must be performed in a certain way, and both you and your dog are judged on your abilities to perform these exercises.

Both the AKC and the UKC sponsor obedience competitions for all breeds of dog, as do some of the breed-specific organizations. There are also independent obedience competitions or tournaments held all over the country.

Before you begin training to compete, write to the sponsoring organization and get a copy of the rules and regulations pertaining to competitions. Go to a few local dog shows and watch the obedience competitions. See who wins and who doesn't. What did they do differently?

If you admire the fluffy, well-groomed look of show dogs, you should consider using a hair dryer on your dog for after his bath. Start using it when he's a pup so he will learn to enjoy the experience. Photo courtesy of Metropolitan Vacuum Cleaner Co., Inc.

There are also a number of books on the market specifically addressing obedience competition. You may want to find a trainer in your area who specializes in competition training.

Canine Good Citizen

The Canine Good Citizen (CGC) program was instituted by the AKC in an effort to promote and reward responsible dog ownership. During a CGC test, the dog and owner must complete a series of ten exercises, including sitting for petting and grooming, walking nicely on the leash, and demonstrating the basic commands sit, down, stay, and come. Upon the successful completion of all ten exercises, the dog is awarded the title

Springers are known for their athletic ability. The tire jump is one of the many activities included in the agility competition in which Springers can excel.

"CGC." For more information about CGC tests, contact a dog trainer or dog training club in your area.

Temperament Test

The American Temperament Test Society was founded to provide breeders and trainers with a means of uniformly evaluating a dog's temperament using standardized tests. The tests can be used to evaluate potential or future breeding stock, future working dogs, or simply as a way for dog owners to see how their dog might

---

FLYBALL

Flyball is a great sport for dogs who are crazy about tennis balls. Teams of four dogs and their owners compete against each other. The dogs—one per team at a time—run down the course, jump four hurdles, and then trigger a mechanism that spits out a tennis ball. The dogs catch the ball, turn, jump the four hurdles again, and return to their owner. The first team to complete the relay wins. Flyball is a fun sport, and many Springers have done well in it.

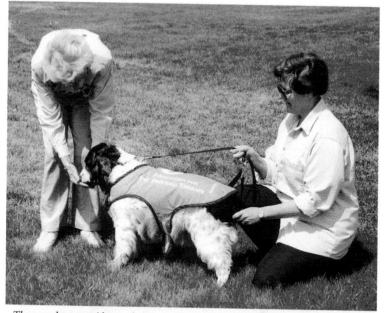

Therapy dogs provide people in nursing homes, hospitals, and children's centers with love and affection. A Springer is an excellent choice for a therapy dog.

react in any given situation. For information about temperament tests in your area, contact a local trainer or dog training club.

Therapy Dogs

Dog owners have known for years that our dogs are good for us, but now researchers are agreeing that dogs are good medicine. Therapy dogs go to nursing homes, hospitals, and children's centers to provide warmth, affection, and love to the people who need it most. Springers make great therapy dogs. For more information,

contact your dog trainer or local humane organization for information about a group in your area.

Field Trials

Springers were originally field dogs, bred to flush and retrieve birds. Many Springers are still treasured hunting dogs, both for sport and to provide food for the table. The English Springer Spaniel Field Trial Association governs Springer field trials. If you're interested, join a local Springer club in your area, and the members can help you get started.

Have Some
FUN
With Your Training

Retrieving games can be great fun as well as good exercise. Make sure that you praise your Springer enthusiastically when he brings the toy back to you.

As has been mentioned many times before, Springers like to have fun. Combining training with play is one way to make sure your Springer enjoys his training. When your dog enjoys his training, he will be more apt to follow the training voluntarily, which means he will observe your rules.

RETRIEVING

Most Springers like to retrieve, and retrieving games can be great fun as well as good exercise. If your Springer likes to retrieve, all you need to do is get him to bring you back the toy. When you throw the toy and he goes after it, wait until he picks it up. Once he has it in his mouth, call him back to you with a happy tone of voice. If he drops the toy, send him back to it. If he brings the toy all the way back to you, praise him enthusiastically.

Don't let him play tug of war with the toy. If he grabs it and doesn't want to let go, reach over the top of his muzzle and tell him "Give," as you press his top lip against his teeth. You don't have to use much pressure, just enough so that he opens his mouth to relieve the pressure. When he gives you the toy, praise him.

If your Springer likes to take the toy and run with it, let him drag his long line behind him while he plays. Then, when he dashes off, you can step on the line and stop him. Once you've stopped him, call him back to you.

Retrieving games can include retrieving the tennis ball, a Frisbee™, or a number of other toys. Just make sure the ball is big enough that your dog can't choke on it or swallow it, and that the toy is safe and won't hurt your dog when he catches it.

THE NAME GAME

The name game is a great way to make the dog think. (And don't doubt for a minute that your Springer can think!) When you teach your Springer the names of a variety of things around the house, you can then put him to work, too. Tell him to pick up your keys, your purse, or the remote control to the television. The possibilities are unlimited.

Start with two items that are very different, perhaps a tennis ball and a magazine. Sit on the floor with your Springer and place the two items in front of

Teach your Springer to play the "touch it" game. Have a ball in one hand and some treats in the other. The object of the game is to get your dog to touch the ball on his own.

you. Ask him, "Where's the ball?" and bounce the ball so that he tries to grab it or at least pays attention to it. When he touches it, praise him and give him a treat.

When he is responding to the ball, lay it on the floor and send him after it. Praise and reward him. Now set several different items out with the magazine and ball and send him after the ball again. When he is doing well, start all over again with one of his toys. When he will get his toy, put the toy and his ball together and send him after one or the other. Don't correct him if he makes a mistake, just take the toy away from him and try it again. Remember, he's learning a foreign language (yours) at the same time that he's trying to figure out what the game is, so be patient.

TOUCH IT

Have some good treats in one hand and a tennis ball in the other. Tell your dog "Touch it!" and touch the ball to his nose. Take it away quickly, before he can grab it, and give him a treat. Repeat this until he starts moving toward the ball when you say "Touch it." Then put the ball away, and hold your palm open and flat to your dog as you tell him "Touch it."

Touch his nose with your palm and give him a treat. You are trying to teach your dog that "Touch it" means touch your nose to this object.

When he will touch your palm with his nose, start holding your hand in different places within reach of the dog's nose—left, right, up, and down. When he will do this quickly

Teaching your dog how to shake hands is one the oldest and best tricks in the book.

and enthusiastically, get out some of the toys he learned to recognize in the name game and have him touch (not retrieve) some of those by name. Tell him to "Touch the ball!" or "Touch my keys!"

I even taught one of my dogs to touch Squirt, one of our cats. I would tell her, "Touch Squirt!" She would dash up to the cat, nose her gently in the face, and then dash back to me for her treat.

This game can be a lot of fun because your dog is not picking up items that could then be broken or chewed. The dog can also touch items too big to be picked up. With imagination, you can teach your dog the names of a number of different things (your car, for example) and then tell your dog to touch them.

THE COME GAME FOR PUPPIES

Two family members can sit on the ground or floor across the yard or down the hallway from each other. Each should have some treats for the puppy. One family member calls the puppy across the yard or down the hall and when the puppy reaches her, she praises the puppy and gives him a treat. She turns the puppy around so that he's facing the other family member, who then calls the puppy. This very simple game can make teaching the come command exciting for the puppy. In addition, kids can play this game with the puppy, giving them a chance to participate in the puppy's training.

FIND IT

When the dog can identify a few items by name, you can start hiding those items so that he can search for them. For example, once he knows the word "keys," you can drop your keys on the floor under an end table next to the sofa. Tell your Springer, "Find my keys!" and help him look. Ask, "Where are they?" and move him toward the end table. When he finds them, praise him enthusiastically!

As he gets better, make the game more challenging. Make him search in more than one room. Have the item hiding in plain sight or underneath something else. In the beginning, help him when he appears confused. But don't let him give up—make sure he succeeds.

HIDE-AND-SEEK

Start by having a family member pet your Springer, offer him a treat and then go to another room. Tell your Springer, "Find Dad!" and let him go. If he runs right to Dad, praise him! Have different family members play the game, and teach the dog each of their names so that he can search for each family member by name.

As he gets better at the game, the family member hiding will no longer have to pet the dog at the beginning of the game, he can simply go hide.

As long as you provide your Springer with the proper care and attention, he will do anything to please you.

his paw to your hand, but pull your hand away so that he's waving. Praise him. Eventually, you want him to lift his paw higher than for the shake and move it up and down so he looks like he's waving. You can do that with the movements of your hand as he reaches for it. Praise him enthusiastically when he does it right. When he understands the wave, you can stop your hand movements.

Help your dog initially so that he can succeed at the game, but encourage him, too, to use his nose and his scenting abilities.

SHAKE HANDS

Shaking hands is a very easy trick to teach. Have your dog sit in front of you. Reach behind one front paw and as you say, "Shake!" tickle his leg in the hollow just behind his paw. When he lifts his paw, shake it gently and praise him. When he starts lifting his paw on his own, stop tickling.

WAVE

When your dog is shaking hands reliably, tell him "Shake. Wave!" and instead of shaking his paw, reach toward it without taking it. Let him touch

HAVE FUN WITH TRICKS

I taught one of my dogs to play dead, and we both had a lot of fun with it. Michi got so good that he could pick the phrase "dead dog" out of casual conversation. One day, the son of a neighbor of mine had just graduated from the police academy and was very proud of his new uniform. Michi and I were out front, so we went over to congratulate the new police officer. As I shook the police officer's hand, I turned to Michi and asked him, "Would you rather be a cop or a dead dog?" Michi dropped to the ground, went flat on his side, and closed his eyes. The only thing giving away that he really was having fun was the wagging tail. Meanwhile, my neighbor's son was stuttering and turning red. He didn't know whether to be offended or to laugh. It was great fun!

Because of their energetic nature, Springers need to exercise on a daily basis. Make exercising fun by making up different activities and games.

Photo by Isabelle Francais

ROLL OVER

With your Springer lying down, take a treat and make a circle with your hand around his nose as you tell him, "Roll over." Use the treat (in the circular motion) to lead his head in the direction you want him to roll. Your other hand may have to help him. Once he knows "roll over," teach him to count. Tell him "Two rollovers" and help him roll over two times. Tell him "Three rollovers" and help him do it three times. Any more than three may make him dizzy. However, you can impress your friends when they think your dog can count to three.

MAKE UP YOUR OWN TRICKS

What would you and your Springer have fun doing? Teach him to stand up on his back legs and dance. Teach him to jump through a hula hoop or your arms forming a circle. Teach him to play dead or to sneeze. Trick training is limited only by your imagination and your ability to teach your dog.
